The Power of Words

Harnessing Divine Communication for Impactful Relationships

By

Daniel Meguille

© Copyright 2025 Daniel Meguille. All rights reserved.

It is illegal to reproduce, duplicate or transmit any part of this document in either electronic means or printed format. Recording of this publication is strictly prohibited.

Dedication

To my beloved wife, **Audrey Meguille Soyam** -
your love, prayers, and steadfast faith have been a constant source of strength. You embody **Proverbs 31:26:** *"She opens her mouth with wisdom, and the teaching of kindness is on her tongue."*

To my precious children - **Victory, Daniel, Angel, and Matthew Meguille Soyam** -
you are gifts from the Lord, each with a divine calling. My prayer for you echoes *Ephesians 4:29: "Do not let any unwholesome talk come out of your mouths, but only what is helpful for building others up."*

To my dear brother, **Samuel Soyam** -
your encouragement, friendship, and unwavering belief in me have been a blessing beyond words. May you always stand on the promise of *Proverbs 18:21: "Death and life are in the power of the tongue, and those who love it will eat its fruit."*

To my valued colleague, **Anita Muca** -
thank you for standing by me with loyalty, support, and a steadfast heart in moments that mattered most. Your strength and faith remind me of *Proverbs 27:17: "As iron sharpens iron, so one person sharpens another."*

May this book remind each of you - my family, my brother, and my colleague - that words have the power to bless, to heal, and to bring life. Always speak with truth, grace, and love, and let your voice glorify God in every season of life.

Contents

Preface 1
Foreword 3
The Marvellous Anatomy of Words 5
   The Roots of Communication 5
   The Divine Tapestry of Language 12
   Connecting Through Expression 20
Seeds of Light: Harnessing Faith Through Speech 29
   Illuminating Conversations 29
   Nurturing Positive Dialogue 37
   Transforming Challenging Relationships 44
   Tending to Weeds of Doubt 46
   Replacing Negativity with Faith-Filled Affirmations 52
   Cultivating Healthy and Fruitful Dialogue 55
Amplified Echoes: Shaping Identity Through Words ... 57
   Colouring Our Narratives 57
   The Power of Affirmation 65
   Narratives of Transformation 73
Tidal Waves or Gentle Breezes? The Impact of Our Conversations 81
   The Forces of Dialogue 81
   Creating Safe Spaces 88
   Practical Strategies for Creating Safe Spaces 90
   The Role of Faith in Creating Safe Spaces 96

    The Ripple Effect 98

Speak Life: The Essence of Encouragement 106

    The Biblical Foundation of Encouragement 106

    Crafting Words of Life 113

    Understanding the Impact of Words 114

    Specific Phrases to Inspire 117

    Building an Arsenal of Words 119

    The Power of Context in Communication 120

    Harnessing the Divine in Our Daily Speech 121

    Conclusion: Embracing the Journey of Crafting Words 121

Harbours of Harmony: Navigating Conflict Through
Communication 129

    Anchoring Empathy 129

    The Art of Deliberate Speech 136

    The Foundation of Deliberate Speech 137

    Recognising Emotional Triggers 138

    Practising Active Listening 139

    Choosing Words Wisely 140

    The Pause Principle 140

    Empathising with the Other Party 141

    The Role of Nonverbal Communication 142

    Reframing Conflict as Opportunity 142

    Creating a Culture of Deliberate Speech 143

    Building Bridges, Not Walls 145

In Tune with the Divine: God's Word as the Ultimate Guide 152
  Listening for Divine Guidance 152
  Scriptural Insights on Communication 159
  Living Out the Word Daily 166
Mirrors of the Soul: Reflecting Love Through Dialogue 175
  Understanding Self through Communication 175
  God's Image in Our Words 184
  Cultivating Relationships Through Love 192
A Journey Beyond Words: Feelings and the Art of Listening.... 202
  The Landscape of Listening 202
  The Essence of Listening 203
  Components of Active Listening 203
  Challenges to Active Listening 207
  Cultivating the Art of Listening 207
  The Transformative Power of Listening 209
  Empathy: The Heart of Listening 211
  Engaging in Communion 219
Beyond Sound: Truly Living the Power of Words 227
  Integrating Insights into Daily Life 227
  Reflect and Review 228
  Mindful Engagement 228
  Harness the Power of Affirmation 229
  Create a Culture of Openness 230
  Engage in Regular Check-Ins 231

Embrace Opportunities for Vulnerability 232
Align Your Words with Your Actions 232
Cultivate Group Conversations 233
Utilise Social Media with Intention 233
Commit to Lifelong Learning 234
A Call to Action 235
Embodying Transformative Practices 236
Conclusion 243
A Call to Action 244

Preface

Dear Reader,

Welcome to a journey into one of the most extraordinary gifts we possess: ***The Power of the Word.***

From the beginning of creation, words have held the power to shape reality. God spoke, and the universe came into being. Every sentence we utter, every thought we give voice to, carries the potential to build up or tear down, to heal or to wound, to inspire or to discourage. This truth has fascinated me for years and inspired the writing of this book.

This is not just a reflection on language; it is an exploration of the spiritual, emotional, and practical force hidden within every word we speak. Words are not empty sounds — they are seeds, capable of producing life or death in the hearts of those who hear them. Scripture reminds us that **"death and life are in the power of the tongue"** (Proverbs 18:21), and it is this divine principle that lies at the heart of these pages.

As I wrote, I desired to create something that would not only open your eyes to the weight of your words but also equip you to use them with purpose, love, and wisdom. I wanted to blend biblical truths with real-life stories, personal experiences, and practical insights so that you can see both the beauty and the responsibility that come with speech.

Throughout this book, we will explore how words can bless, heal, encourage, and guide — as well as how careless words can harm, divide, and destroy. You will see how God's Word offers the perfect model for truth-filled, grace-saturated communication, and how you can reflect that in your own life.

My prayer is that as you read, you will be inspired to speak life into every situation, to harness the creative and redemptive power of your words, and to align your speech with the heart of God.

So open these pages with expectation. May what you discover here transform not only your vocabulary but your entire way of living.

With every blessing,

Daniel Meguille

Foreword

Words are among the most potent forces in the world. They can create and they can destroy; they can breathe life into a weary soul or crush a spirit in an instant. From the very beginning, the Bible teaches us that God spoke creation into existence. With His Word, light pierced the darkness, order came from chaos, and life began. That same God-given gift — the ability to speak — remains one of the most profound ways we influence the world around us.

The Power of the Word is more than a reflection on language; it is a guide to recognising and harnessing this God-given ability with wisdom, love, and purpose. Through its pages, you will see how words can heal wounds, build bridges, restore hope, and reveal truth. You will also see how careless or destructive words can sow discord, wound hearts, and hinder growth.

The author does not simply present theory; he invites you into a personal and spiritual journey — one that blends biblical truth, life experience, and practical steps to help you align your words with God's will. Every chapter challenges you to examine what you speak, why you say it, and how it shapes the lives of those around you.

The Power of Words

This book is written with the author's heart laid bare, dedicated to those he loves most — his wife, **Audrey, and their children, *Victory, Daniel, Angel, and Matthew*.** It is also written for you, the reader, with the hope that you will finish these pages inspired to speak life, truth, and grace into every conversation.

As you read, remember this: the words you speak today will echo in the hearts of others tomorrow. Let them be words worth remembering.

The Marvellous Anatomy of Words

The Roots of Communication

In the intricate dance of human interaction, words serve not merely as tools for communication but as the very roots that nourish our relationships. Words, like the unseen roots of a majestic tree, lie beneath the surface and often go unnoticed. Yet, their strength and resilience shape the trunk of our communication, providing stability and sustenance to our connections. To understand the power of words, one must first delve into their etymology and the fundamental elements that form the essence of our verbal exchanges.

Etymology, the study of the origin of words and how their meanings have evolved, reveals profound insights into the nature of language itself. When we trace the lineage of a word, we uncover layers of history, culture, and belief that give it depth and significance. For instance, consider the word 'communication,' which originates from the Latin verb 'communicare,' meaning 'to share' or 'to make common.' This root highlights the core purpose of communication: the act of sharing thoughts, feelings, and ideas to create a sense of community.

The Power of Words

Every word carries its own history, enriching our understanding of how it connects us to others. The word 'love,' for example, has roots in Old English as 'lufu,' embodying both affection and a profound commitment to another. Throughout history, love has been expressed in countless languages, in myriad ways, yet it consistently serves as a bridge between souls. By comprehending the etymology of words, we begin to see how they hold the power to reflect our innermost emotions, and in doing so, foster connections that transcend the mundane.

Language has often been compared to the roots of an ancient tree because, much like those roots, it goes deep into the rich soil of our human experience. The roots of a tree anchor it firmly in place, providing nourishment and support while allowing it to grow tall and strong. Similarly, the words we choose to communicate with anchor us in our relationships and determine how we nurture those bonds. Just as roots intertwine and support each other underground, our words can weave a tapestry of connection that enriches our lives.

The connection to nature is not merely poetic; it is a reflection of a greater truth. The roots of language reach deep into the earth, collecting nutrients from the varied experiences of human existence. Whether it is the language of love shared between partners, the comforting words of a friend, or the affirmations that build community, each interaction nourishes the soul. As we share words of encouragement, wisdom, or empathy, we are, in essence, watering the roots of our relationships. We must be mindful of what we say, as the nourishment we provide can either foster growth or contribute to decay.

As we ponder these analogies, we must also recognise the divine significance embedded in language. The Scriptures teach us that 'In the beginning was the Word, and the Word was with God, and the Word was God' (John 1:1). This profound statement illustrates the foundational role of words in the divine narrative. God spoke the universe into existence through His words, demonstrating that creation itself is rooted in communication. The power of words lies not only in their ability to express thought but also in their capacity to affect change, evoke emotion, and ultimately shape the world around us.

Our capacity to convey our beliefs and emotions through language elevates us beyond mere creatures of instinct. We have the divine gift of articulation, enabling us to share our faith and love in tangible ways. Words serve as a medium, allowing us to express the depths of our longing for connection with both God and one another. Without words, our understanding of spirituality would remain limited and inaccessible, unable to weave it into existence through the intricate dance of language.

The Power of Words

As we explore the roots of communication, it becomes essential to consider how language has evolved alongside humanity. From the earliest forms of guttural sounds to the complex languages we use today, words have undergone significant transformation. Each shift in language reflects the societal and cultural dynamics of its time, highlighting the adaptability of human expression.

Consider, for example, how different cultures have developed unique expressions of gratitude and reverence. The word 'thank you' varies not only in pronunciation but also in sentiment across languages. In Japanese, 'arigatou' is rooted in the concept of gratitude for the effort expended by another. This cultural nuance conveys a richer understanding of what it means to appreciate others, reminding us that our words must align with our intentions.

Throughout history, languages have borrowed from one another, enriched by cross-cultural exchanges that expand vocabulary and meaning. This evolution of language showcases the necessity of adaptability in communication. Just as the roots of a tree stretch and grow in response to their environment, so too must our words morph to reflect the multicultural tapestry of our world, allowing for deeper connections across varying backgrounds.

In today's global society, the necessity for effective communication is more vital than ever. With the rise of technology, the distance that once separated us has diminished, leading to a cacophony of voices and influences. Yet, amidst this noise, we must remain intentional about our words. Mindful communication fosters understanding and acceptance while bridging the gaps created by cultural, linguistic, and ideological differences. As we cultivate our relationships, let us approach communication as a sacred act, one that should be infused with care and consideration.

Equipped with the realisation of the roots of communication, we embark on a journey to develop meaningful connections in our lives. Each conversation presents an opportunity to nourish relationships, much like a gardener tending to a garden. Just as roots draw sustenance from the earth, we must actively listen and engage with those around us, absorbing their thoughts and feelings as a way to foster a sense of belonging. The act of listening carefully to others' words symbolises our commitment to understanding their perspectives.

Furthermore, we must recognise the uniqueness of each person's linguistic roots. Just as roots grow in varied soils, our experiences shape the way we communicate. Cultural backgrounds, familial influences, and personal histories all contribute to the development of our distinctive voices. By acknowledging the diverse roots from which our words emerge, we cultivate empathy and respect in our interactions.

The Power of Words

Our language not only shapes the way we express ourselves but also influences the way we perceive the world. Research has shown that the languages we speak can influence our thoughts and behaviours. For instance, languages with rich descriptive vocabulary about relationships promote stronger social bonds compared to those lacking such terms—the words we choose frame our reality, colouring our perceptions and shaping our identities. The choice to speak life or negativity reflects the roots from which we draw our strength.

The roots of communication also ground us in accountability. When we speak, we must carry the weight of our words—a weight that can uplift or tear down. As Christians, we are called to be stewards of our language, using it as a tool to reflect the divine love that resides within us. Our words are charged with the capability to heal wounds or sow discord, and thus we must approach them with reverence. The Bible emphasises the importance of speaking truthfully and encouragingly, reminding us that 'the tongue has the power of life and death' (Proverbs 18:21). We must be diligent in choosing words that affirm, inspire, and uplift.

Moreover, as the roots of a tree burrow deep into the earth to draw life-sustaining water, so too must we root ourselves in the source of life: God's Word. The Scriptures present a blueprint for wholesome communication, offering timeless and transformative guidance. By immersing ourselves in God's teachings, we cultivate a deeper understanding of how to navigate our conversations with grace and love.

In examining the roots of communication, we also must appreciate the importance of authenticity. Each word we utter should resonate with the truth of our hearts. In an era where communication often feels superficial, we are called to dig deeper, acknowledging our vulnerabilities while remaining transparent in our dialogue. Authentic communication builds trust, fostering relationships that are not merely based on appearances but grounded in shared understanding and mutual respect.

Consider the way the roots of a tree intertwine, providing support and strength not just to one tree but the entire forest. Likewise, our words may serve as a metaphorical root system for those around us. When we choose to speak words of kindness and affirmation, we empower others and encourage them to flourish. Just as a tree contributes to its ecosystem, our communication can nurture entire communities, reflecting the love of Christ in tangible ways.

Ultimately, the roots of communication extend beyond the mere mechanical act of speaking. They delve into the depths of our hearts, intertwining with our values, beliefs, and experiences. Words are seeds that bear fruit, and as we thoughtfully cultivate them in our relationships, we yield a bounty of connection, love, and understanding.

As we journey forward in our exploration of the marvellous anatomy of words, let us remain anchored in the recognition of their divine power. The words we choose to wield have the ability to shape not only our identities but also the world around us. As we articulate our thoughts, let our language become a beacon of hope, love, and faith that nourishes not only our souls but those of others. Just as the roots of an ancient tree reach deep and wide, let us nurture our words and relationships, allowing them to flourish in the beauty of divine connection.

The Divine Tapestry of Language

In the beginning, God spoke, and from His words, the universe sprang into existence. This divine act of communication set a profound precedent, demonstrating that words are not mere sequences of sounds but vessels of creation, intention, and divine purpose. Language, both written and spoken, is a sacred tapestry woven through history, cultures, and generations. It serves as the medium through which humanity connects, shares experiences, and communicates the essence of life itself.

The Power of Words

To understand the divine tapestry of language, we must first recognise the multifaceted nature of communication. Language is enriched by its roots, shaped by culture, and designed for connection. This intricate mosaic is both an art form and a spiritual journey, allowing believers to express their faith and experiences in relatable ways. As we delve deeper into this exploration, we will uncover scriptural references that celebrate communication as a divine creation, urging readers to recognise the sacredness of the words they use in their everyday lives.

Written language has been the cornerstone of human expression, enabling the recording of thoughts, stories, and divine revelations. The scriptures themselves highlight numerous instances where the written word played a significant role in conveying God's message to His people. From the tablets of stone given to Moses, inscribed with the Ten Commandments, to the letters of Paul addressing early Christian communities, written communication has played a pivotal role in shaping faith. Each instance reminds us that words are not static; they carry the weight of history, commitment, and divine truth.

The spoken word, too, holds immeasurable power. Jesus, the Living Word, communicated profound truths through parables and teachings that resonated with the hearts of His listeners. His words were imbued with life, healing, and transformation, providing a blueprint for believers today on how to engage others through spoken communication. In conversations marked by grace and compassion, we reflect the essence of Christ, creating opportunities for connection, understanding, and mutual support.

Within these two realms of language lies the beauty of expression. Each word chosen has the potential to uplift or to discourage, to build bridges or erect barriers. In examining this dynamic interplay, we can draw from the wisdom found in Proverbs 18:21, which states, 'The tongue has the power of life and death, and those who love it will eat its fruit.' This scripture emphasises the impact of our words, urging us to approach communication with reverence and intentionality.

As we navigate the complexities of language, it is essential to remember that our communication practices should reflect our values and beliefs. The essence of God's Word teaches us that communication is not merely about transmission, but about connection. Human beings are created in the image of God, and just as He used words to create and communicate, we too are endowed with the capacity to shape our reality through our speech. This invites us to adopt a divinely inspired approach to self-expression.

In the Gospels, we witness Jesus consistently seeking to communicate with clarity and purpose. He understood the cultural context of His listeners and tailored His messages to resonate deeply with their lives. His ability to discern the needs of those around Him allowed Him to speak into their circumstances with empathy and love. As followers of Christ, we are called to do the same, engaging with others in a manner that honours their experiences and fosters meaningful dialogue.

The impact of language is further evidenced throughout the Bible, where it is characterised as a dual-edged sword—capable of cutting through deception while also providing healing and hope. The book of Hebrews states, 'For the word of God is alive and active. Sharper than any double-edged sword, it penetrates even to dividing soul and spirit, joints and marrow; it judges the thoughts and attitudes of the heart' (Hebrews 4:12). Here, the emphasis on the vitality of words invites us to consider the spiritual weight they carry.

To appreciate this sacred power fully, we must recognise the role of intention in our communication. Every conversation, whether casual or significant, is an opportunity to affirm, challenge, and support one another in our journeys of faith. The Apostle Paul instructs us in Ephesians 4:29, saying, 'Do not let any unwholesome talk come out of your mouths, but only what helps build others up according to their needs, that it may benefit those who listen.' This extraction highlights the importance of intentional language that fosters growth rather than division, promoting a culture of encouragement within our communities.

As we examine language within the context of faith, we uncover the rich tapestry of words that echo throughout scripture. From Genesis to Revelation, language serves as a medium through which God reveals Himself, encourages His people, and offers wisdom. Consider the poetic beauty of the Psalms, where David's heartfelt expressions of worship and lament invite us into an intimate conversation with God. His words give voice to our deepest desires, sorrows, and joys, reminding us that our spoken and written language can be a form of prayer—an offering of our thoughts and emotions to the divine.

The narrative of redemption woven into the fabric of the scriptures employs language as a powerful tool for transformation. God's promises articulated through the prophets serve as a reminder of His commitment to humanity. These words are steeped in hope and the promise of restoration, revealing a God who desires a relationship with His creation. The book of Isaiah presents a poignant testament to this idea: 'The grass withers and the flowers fall, but the word of our God endures forever' (Isaiah 40:8). Here, we are reminded that while earthly things may fade, the divine Word remains constant and ever relevant.

The Power of Words

In addition to the references to divine communication in scripture, we must also recognise the nonverbal cues and the complexities of context in our spoken interactions. Language is not only what we articulate verbally; our body language, tone, and demeanour contribute significantly to the message we convey. This holistic view of communication reminds us that we are always 'speaking'—even when we are silent. To truly embody the essence of divine communication, we must acknowledge that our presence and our actions are intertwined with the words we choose to express.

Cultivating an awareness of our communication practices can lead to a more profound understanding of the impact our speech can have on the lives of others. The humble, mindful use of language reflects the heart of God's message to the world: that we are called to love, support, and uplift one another. Through this lens, we can discern our role in a tapestry that extends beyond ourselves—the interconnectedness of all relationships reinforces the importance of speaking life and encouraging one another.

As we appreciate the divine tapestry of language, let us also consider the significance of storytelling within the fabric of communication. Stories have the power to evoke emotions, inspire hope, and instil a sense of belonging. The parables of Jesus, rich in cultural context and wisdom, serve as timeless examples, demonstrating how narratives can convey profound theological truths while engaging the hearts and minds of listeners. Stories not only express ideas but also forge connections between the teller and the audience, reminding us that our experiences can resonate with others in profoundly meaningful ways.

In light of this understanding, we should strive to engage in conversations that invite stories—both our own and those of others. As we listen and share, we create an atmosphere where vulnerability can exist and where the power of words can inspire growth and healing. Each narrative we encounter has the potential to weave itself into the larger tapestry, further reflecting the diversity and richness of the human experience within the context of God's love.

While the exploration of written and spoken language reveals the beauty of divine communication, we must also acknowledge the importance of discernment in our expression. Not all language conveys truth; thus, we must cultivate an awareness of the words we choose. In 1 Thessalonians 5:21, Paul exhorts believers, 'Test all things; hold fast what is good.' This reminder underscores the necessity of filtering our language through the lens of faith, ensuring that our communication aligns with the principles of love, kindness, and truth.

As we engage with those around us, we can embrace a spirit of humility that recognises our limits. Before we speak, let us take a moment to reflect on the potential consequences of our words. Will they build trust? Will they reflect our Christian values? Are they rooted in love? Such intentionality allows us to embody the essence of Christ-centred communication, and as we do so, the divine tapestry of language is woven even more beautifully.

Our journey through the divine tapestry of language reveals the ethereal nature of words and the sacred responsibility attached to their articulation. As believers, we are called to recognise that our communication serves not only as a means of connection but also as an avenue for empowerment. Just as God's Word nourishes our souls, our words can uplift and inspire those around us. Consider the words of Proverbs 12:18, 'The words of the reckless pierce like swords, but the tongue of the wise brings healing.' This illustrates the profound impact of language and the importance of making informed choices.

In conclusion, the divine tapestry of language is a rich and complex reflection of our journey as communicators. As we navigate the intricacies of speech and writing, let us be mindful of the words we choose, anchoring our language in the principles of faith and love. Through the threads of spoken and written communication, we can build bridges, foster relationships, and reflect the heart of God to the world. May we always strive to engage others with intentionality, recognising the profound beauty embedded within the words we speak and share, creating a tapestry that is vibrant, life-giving, and reflective of His divine purpose.

Connecting Through Expression

In the intricate dance of human interaction, the words we choose to express our thoughts and feelings hold immeasurable power. Genuine expressions not only articulate our internal landscapes but also serve as bridges that allow us to connect with others on a profound level. This connection is essential for building trust and deepening relationships, and yet it is often overlooked in the hustle and bustle of daily life. To truly connect through expression, we must delve deeply into the elements of authenticity, clarity, and intention behind our words.

When we strive to communicate genuinely, we set the stage for meaningful exchanges that invite understanding rather than misunderstanding. Authentic expressions are those that come from a place of truth, drawn from our core values and emotions. It's important to recognise that authenticity is not merely about honesty in our statements but also about conveying our feelings and intentions in a way that others can resonate with.

Consider the story of Julia and Mark. They were colleagues who had worked together for a few years, their interactions primarily limited to work-related discussions. While they enjoyed a cordial professional relationship, an underlying tension remained, an invisible wall that separated them.

One day, during a team meeting, Mark received harsh criticism from their manager. Observing Mark's discomfort, Julia felt an urge to reach out beyond the surface of their professional facades. After the meeting, she approached him with a genuine concern in her tone. 'I noticed that the feedback upset you,' she said softly. Julia's words were laden with authenticity, reflecting her true feelings without any agenda. She wasn't simply being polite; she was expressing genuine empathy.

Mark looked taken aback but then nodded, the corner of his mouth twitching up in what could be interpreted as a reluctant smile. 'It caught me off guard. I always put in my best effort, and I suppose I'm not used to such blunt feedback,' he confessed. This exchange became a pivotal moment for both of them. Julia's authenticity encouraged Mark to share his feelings, something he had otherwise been reluctant to do. This moment of vulnerability opened a door for deeper trust to blossom.

Authenticity prompts us to express not only the happy or comfortable thoughts but also the challenging ones. When we speak our truth, we create space for others to reflect on their experiences and emotions in a relatable way. This mutual sharing fosters an environment where genuine connections can flourish.

Clarity accompanies authenticity as a vital component of effective communication. It isn't enough to communicate honestly; our thoughts and feelings also need to be communicated in a way that is clear and comprehensible to the recipient. Without clarity, even the most heartfelt intentions can be misconstrued, leading to confusion or, worse, conflict.

Recall the story of Brian and his friend Lisa, who had been close for years. One day, Brian felt compelled to express his thoughts after Lisa had confided in him about a personal issue. He crafted what he believed was a supportive message, encouraging her to seek help. However, despite his good intentions, the message became convoluted due to his mixed metaphors and vague references.

Lisa, who read the text with a furrowed brow, felt misunderstood and unappreciated. 'I thought you would be more supportive instead of just telling me what to do,' she reacted defensively.

In this instance, Brian's authentic intention collided with a lack of clarity. The meaning of his words got lost in translation. To foster trust and understanding, it's essential that we not only express our thoughts honestly but also articulate them clearly and effectively.

This alignment between intent and clarity allows our words to resonate with the listener, bridging gaps that may otherwise exist.

Intention plays a crucial role in forging connections through expression. Actions and words grounded in authentic intention hold an even greater weight than expressions created out of obligation or routine. As we reflect on our communication habits, we must ask ourselves what we hope to achieve through our words. Are we seeking to uplift, connect, clarify, or simply pass the time?

Let's dive back into Julia and Mark's evolving relationship. Their candid conversation after the meeting not only opened the door to trust but also laid the foundation for a mutually supportive friendship. They began to share personal anecdotes during lunch breaks, exploring their dreams, fears, and the challenges they faced in their respective roles.

Julia was intentional about checking in with Mark regularly, asking, 'How's everything going?' Each time she posed the question, the sincerity in her voice made it clear that she was genuinely interested in hearing more than just a surface-level response. Her unwavering intention to foster a supportive environment allowed Mark to feel valued and understood.

This nurturing approach to dialogue inspired Mark to also step outside his comfort zone. His responses grew richer with context, revealing insights into his aspirations and the pressures he faced in their demanding work environment. The evolution of their conversations illustrated how intention served as a catalyst for deeper connection, fortifying the bridge Julia had initially constructed through her authentic expression.

Genuine expressions also necessitate vulnerability, a powerful element often disregarded in conventional social interactions. To express ourselves genuinely, we must be willing to expose our thoughts and emotions, even when they make us feel uncomfortable. This does not mean laying our entire emotional state bare at every opportunity; instead, it involves choosing moments of vulnerability that foster authentic connections.

Mark, spurred on by Julia's openness, decided to share an instance where he had struggled to balance his work and personal life. In sharing, he revealed feelings of inadequacy and the fear of disappointing his loved ones. This act of vulnerability prompted Julia to share her own experiences of juggling responsibilities and the weight that came with them. Such exchanges build enduring bonds, as both individuals find common ground in their shared experiences.

As the rapport between Julia and Mark flourished, they became each other's sounding boards, proving that genuine expression transcended superficial interaction. Their conversations evolved from merely discussing work projects to discussing their personal lives, aspirations, and realisations about themselves. This transformation demonstrated that authentic dialogue, driven by clarity and intention, bolsters relationships amidst life's complexities.

Yet, while striving for connection through our expressions, we must also be mindful of the potential for miscommunication. Words, while powerful, are delicate, often influenced by context and personal circumstances. Recognising the potential for misunderstanding is essential; it empowers us to take steps towards clearer, more compassionate communication.

Consider the instance of a friend of mine, Sarah, who, during a moment of honest conversation, had intended to uplift her sister, Lila, by offering constructive feedback on a new project she was working on. In her attempts to provide insights, Sarah felt her words, though rooted in care, were received defensively. They had devolved into a heated argument, with Lila feeling attacked rather than supported.

This miscommunication stemmed from Sarah's inability to accurately gauge Lila's emotional state—a gentle touch would have fostered an entirely different response. They ultimately reconciled after dialogue and realising their intent, but the initial impact highlighted how context can significantly influence the reception of our words. This further emphasises the importance of delivering genuine expressions with an acute awareness of the listener's perspective.

As we engage with others, much like Julia and Mark, or Sarah and Lila, we can aim for expressions and conversations that embody clarity, authenticity, and intention. Every conversation holds the potential to be a seed, catalysing relationships that foster understanding and compassion. How we choose to water those seeds—the authenticity we embody, the clarity we offer, and the intentions we uphold—will dictate whether they blossom into robust relationships or shrivel in the shadows of superficiality.

Additionally, embracing the nuance of our words can greatly enhance communication. Misunderstandings can arise from more than just unclear expressions; they can also stem from cultural or personal biases that colour our interpretations. Each individual carries a tapestry of experiences that shapes how they understand and respond to words. To navigate these complexities, engage in active listening and ask open-ended questions that encourage others to share their feelings and interpretations.

The Power of Words

In the spirit of deepening our connections, cultivating an empathetic understanding will allow us to navigate misunderstandings with grace. Recognise that your perspective might not align with someone else's experience. When we acknowledge the validity of others' experiences, we enrich our conversations, creating a dynamic interplay of shared sentiments.

That said, there are practical steps that can empower us to genuinely express ourselves, enhancing our ability to connect through expression. Start with reflection: take time to contemplate your emotions and thoughts before articulating them to others. This conscious approach will not only enhance clarity but also strengthen your connection with the essence of what you wish to convey. By doing so, you will choose words in alignment with your values and intentions, creating a more robust bridge for connection.

Practice active listening in conversations. When engaging with someone, ensure you are fully present and attentive. Practice being mindful not just of what is being said but also how it is being expressed. Reflect what you hear, creating a participatory dialogue where both parties feel acknowledged. This fluid exchange of thoughts and sentiments fosters mutual understanding and cultivates an environment in which genuine expressions can thrive.

The Power of Words

Moreover, encourage meaningful conversations by asking thought-provoking questions. During discussions, instead of defaulting to surface-level inquiries, delve deeper: 'What motivated you to choose that path?' or 'How did that experience shape your views?' Such questions evoke rich narratives, allowing individuals to articulate their emotions and thoughts more authentically. These conversations can lead to revelations and deeper connections as shared experiences surface.

In closing, the journey toward connecting through expression begins with an awareness of the power that lies within our words. Authenticity, clarity, and intention are the pillars that sustain this endeavour. Just as Julia and Mark transformed their acquaintance into a robust friendship, so too can we cultivate meaningful relationships by conscientiously articulating our thoughts and feelings.

As we navigate the complexities of human interactions, let our hearts guide our words, illuminating the pathways that connect us. Through genuine expressions, we can foster enriching relationships that resonate, reminding us of the true potential of the human spirit.

In the end, let us take each opportunity to speak life, sowing seeds of connection that yield trust, understanding, and love across the canvas of our shared existence.

Seeds of Light: Harnessing Faith Through Speech

Illuminating Conversations

In the heart of every meaningful relationship lies the power of conversation. It is through dialogue that we share our thoughts, our aspirations, and at times, our fears. As we engage in conversations, we may not fully realise that the words we choose serve as seeds, planted in the rich soil of our intentions and beliefs. Just as a gardener carefully selects the seeds they wish to plant and grow, we must be intentional about the words we speak, acknowledging that each one has the potential to blossom into vibrant connections or, conversely, become entangled in weeds of doubt and negativity.

Consider, for a moment, the metaphor of a garden. Every seed sown represents an opportunity—an opportunity to nurture a relationship or to let it wither under neglect. Picture the words that flow from your lips as the droplets of rain that nourish your garden. When they are filled with encouragement, kindness, and understanding, they create a fertile ground for relationships to thrive. On the other hand, words that are harsh or dismissive act as choking weeds, inhibiting growth and obscuring the light of true connection.

The Power of Words

In this exploration, we will delve into the principles of illuminating conversations, focusing on how our words can light the way for others while simultaneously enriching our own experiences. Through the lens of faith, we will uncover how language cultivates relationships and illuminates paths, guiding us toward deeper understanding with those we cherish most.

As we embark on this journey, it's crucial to recognise the divine potential of our speech. Words are not just mere sounds; they are reflections of our hearts, embodiments of our faith, and tools for building bridges between souls. In the Bible, numerous references illustrate the significance of our dialogue. Proverbs 18:21 reminds us that 'The tongue has the power of life and death, and those who love it will eat its fruit.' This verse encapsulates the reality that words are powerful currencies in the realm of human interaction. Let us explore how to harness that power for illumination.

The seeds of light are often sown in the fertile ground of active listening. Just as a garden requires attention and care, so too do our conversations. Have you ever engaged in a dialogue where you felt heard, understood, and valued? In those moments, it becomes painfully clear how vital it is to listen attentively. Active listening requires us to focus not only on the words spoken but also on the emotions underlying them. When we take the time to listen, we demonstrate that we value the other person's experience. This act alone can transform a mundane conversation into a beautiful exchange of insights, a dance where both partners contribute to the rhythm of understanding.

Turning our attention to the types of conversations we engage in, we see that illuminating dialogue often includes elements of authenticity and vulnerability. When we share our true selves, we invite others to do the same, thereby deepening our connections and fostering a sense of authenticity. Just as a gardener prunes plants to encourage growth and openness, we can choose to prune our conversations of superficiality and pretence, allowing authenticity to flourish.

For instance, consider a conversation where a friend confides in you about a personal struggle. Instead of offering platitudes or quickly changing the subject to lighten the mood, what if you chose to sit in the discomfort with them? By acknowledging their pain, asking open-ended questions, and allowing silence to settle in, you create an environment rich for growth. It is in these authentic exchanges that bonds are formed and nurtured.

As we engage in illuminating conversations, we must also be mindful of our intentions. Every word spoken carries weight, and our intentions shape the impact they have. When we approach conversations with a desire to uplift, inspire, and connect, our words become vessels transmitting light. Think of the conversations where you have experienced joy from uplifting exchanges. Maybe it was a compliment received at just the right moment or an expression of gratitude that brought warmth to your heart. These instances reflect intentional speech, acting as seeds of positivity in our gardens.

Moreover, conversations thrive in environments where grace abounds. Grace, in its essence, is unmerited favour, a gift we offer each other even when it's undeserved. Inherent in every relationship are moments of misunderstanding and conflict; however, it is how we handle these moments that can either illuminate or obscure paths moving forward. By choosing to respond with grace, we create opportunities for reconciliation and understanding; even the darkest moments can give way to light.

In connections marked by grace, forgiveness can take root. Picture a relationship plagued by past hurts, akin to a garden overrun by thorny weeds. Just as a gardener must remove the weeds to allow the healthy plants to thrive, we must confront the thorns in our conversations. By extending forgiveness—both to ourselves and to others—we create space for growth and healing.

Consider a scenario where two individuals have had a falling out. Harsh words might have been exchanged, obscuring their original intentions for understanding. Yet, through humble dialogue and a willingness to acknowledge their pain, they can transform their conversation into a flourishing space for reconciliation. Here, the seeds of forgiveness planted in the soil of grace can yield a miraculous garden of renewed trust and connection.

Furthermore, illuminating conversations require us to harness the power of affirmation. Just as sunlight nurtures plants, our affirming words can fuel relationships and personal growth. Positive affirmations not only uplift others but can also reinforce our own sense of identity and belonging. In the realm of faith, speaking life into one another is a way of participating in God's creation, sharing light that reflects the goodness and love of our Creator.

A wonderful example comes from the story of Barnabas in the New Testament. Known as the 'Son of Encouragement,' Barnabas played a pivotal role in uplifting the early church. His words were affirmations of faith that illuminated paths for others to follow, inspiring them to grow into their God-given potential. When we choose to speak life into our relationships by affirming others' strengths and gifts, we cultivate an atmosphere where flourishing faith can thrive.

Let's not overlook the role that timing plays in our conversations. Just as a gardener knows when to plant, nurture, and harvest, we must also discern the right moments to speak. Timing can turn an ordinary conversation into a transformative encounter. There are seasons in our relationships, just like those in nature, and our words must mirror that ebb and flow. For example, during moments of crisis or loss, people's hearts crave compassion and understanding. Speaking life during these pivotal times is essential; it can guide an individual from darkness into light.

Moreover, our choice of language can act as a lens that either clarifies or distorts understanding. Words filled with love and faith serve as beacons of clarity in the tumultuous seas of life. However, language steeped in negativity or sarcasm can obscure insights, leaving confusion in its wake. It is in recognising this choice that we wield the profound opportunity to shape experiences through our dialogue.

As we adopt the gardening metaphor, let's also recognise the importance of ongoing growth and learning in our conversations. Just as a garden changes with the seasons, we, too, must adapt and evolve our communication styles based on the dynamics of our relationships. This requires feedback, reflection, and a genuine willingness to grow. One might consider keeping a journal to reflect on conversations, both illuminating and those filled with shadows. Through this reflective practice, we can examine our patterns of speech, identifying areas where we can improve and cultivate a more nourishing dialogue.

The Power of Words

It's essential to remember that illuminating conversations invite growth, not perfection. Each interaction offers us insights that can help us become more mindful communicators. Like a gardener who learns from nature's cycles, we must embrace the unique rhythm of every relationship we engage in. Rather than striving for flawless speech, we safeguard the authenticity that fosters deeper connections.

As we focus on illuminating our conversations, let's also recognise the power of silence. Sometimes, it is the quiet moments of pause in dialogue that allow the light to illuminate even more profoundly. Silence, when employed wisely, can be transformative; it grants space for reflection, allowing the essence of our discussions to settle in. Especially in emotionally charged conversations, allowing for pauses fosters an environment where thoughts can be considered without the pressure of immediate response. In moments of silence, profound insights can emerge, further nourishing the soil of our interactions.

In reflecting on the various elements of illuminating conversations, we must also confront the reality of obscured insights—moments when our dialogues do not resonate or connect as we hope. In life's ebbs and flows, we will inevitably encounter challenges in our communication. Recognising this is vital; it allows us to approach these situations from a place of humility and grace.

When misunderstandings arise, see them as opportunities to grow together rather than obstacles. Rather than blaming or shutting down, we can choose vulnerability. This willingness to confront friction opens the door to richer conversations that illuminate paths previously shrouded in darkness.

Moreover, acknowledging the obstacles we face in communication requires intentionality. Just as a gardener would remove rocks and debris obstructing the soil, we must actively seek to clear the clutter in our words. This means being aware of underlying biases and assumptions that may cloud our understanding. Taking the time to educate ourselves about the perspectives and experiences of others fosters empathy, illuminating our conversations with greater clarity.

In conclusion, illuminating conversations serve as a reminder of the profound impact our words can have in shaping relationships. By cultivating an openness to listen, an authenticity to share, and a grace to forgive, we create spaces where genuine connections can flourish. These dialogue-rich environments inspire both ourselves and others to grow, nurturing friendships and deepening faith. We hold the power to plant seeds of light in our interactions, trusting that God will tend to their growth. As we embark on our journey through life, let us not forget that every conversation offers a unique opportunity to illuminate paths, connecting our hearts in ways that reflect the divine love we are called to share.

Nurturing Positive Dialogue

In our fast-paced world, filled with distractions and noise, the power of our words often goes unappreciated. Yet, the art of communication has the potential to be a transformative force, especially when it is infused with faith and positivity. In the sprawling garden of our relationships, our words are the seeds we plant, and nurturing them with encouragement can yield vibrant blooms of trust, respect, and unconditional love.

To effectively cultivate positive dialogue, one must start by recognising what uplifting speech truly entails. It is not simply the absence of negativity, but rather a conscious choice to express thoughts and feelings that foster growth and connection. Like a gardener tending to his plants, we must tend to our words, ensuring they enrich the soil of our relationships. Let us explore practical techniques to cultivate conversations that uplift and inspire, drawing from biblical teachings that illustrate the transformative essence of supportive words.

The Power of Words

The Power of Intentionality

Intentionality is the cornerstone of positive dialogue. Just as a gardener carefully selects which seeds to plant, we too must be deliberate about the words we choose. Whenever we enter a conversation, we should ask ourselves, 'What is my intention?' Am I aiming to uplift, encourage, and share hope, or am I falling into routine patterns that might not edify?

To foster intentional communication, start with the following strategies:

1. **Set a Positive Mindset:** Before engaging in dialogue, take a moment to cultivate a spirit of positivity. Pray for guidance or reflect on a scripture that inspires hope. When your mindset is anchored in positivity, the words you share are naturally inclined to uplift.

2. **Choose Words Wisely:** Language is powerful. As Proverbs 18:21 states, 'Death and life are in the power of the tongue, and those who love it will eat its fruits.' This means we reap what we sow in our speech. By consciously choosing words that promote life, encouragement, and affirmation, we can greatly impact the emotional climate of our conversations.

3. **Practice Affirmation:** Affirmation is one of the simplest yet most profound ways to nurture positive dialogue. Identify specific

qualities you admire in the person you are communicating with and voice those thoughts. For instance, telling a friend, 'I appreciate how you always listen with empathy', instils a sense of value and recognition that can deepen relationships.

The Role of Listening in Encouragement

Positive dialogue is a two-way street. While speaking uplifting words is essential, genuine listening forms the foundation upon which those words can take root and have a lasting impact. When we listen actively, we demonstrate respect and openness, creating an atmosphere conducive to encouragement. The Bible emphasises the importance of listening in Proverbs 1:5: 'Let the wise hear and increase in learning, and the one who understands obtain guidance.'

To enhance your listening skills:

1. Focus on the speaker: Physically and mentally engage with the person speaking. Avoid distractions, maintain eye contact, and use nods or verbal affirmations, such as 'I see' or 'Go on,' to show that you are present.

2. Reflect: After the speaker shares their thoughts, reflect on what you've heard to ensure understanding. For example, saying, 'So what I'm hearing is that you feel overwhelmed at work, is that correct?' affirms their feelings and encourages further dialogue.

3. Validate Emotions: Encourage openness by validating the speaker's emotions. Phrases like 'It's completely normal to feel that way' let them know their feelings are acknowledged and respected, paving the way for further encouragement.

Building a Culture of Affirmation

To foster an environment where uplifting dialogue flourishes, it is essential to build a culture of affirmation within our relationships. Communities, whether at home, in church, or at work, thrive when encouragement is baked into the fabric of interactions.

Practical Techniques for Establishing a Culture of Affirmation

1. Regular Check-Ins: Create a routine where individuals can share their experiences and feelings in a supportive environment. Whether it's a family dinner, a church group, or a workplace meeting, dedicate time for open conversations where everyone feels valued and respected.

2. Celebrate Accomplishments: Publicly recognise achievements, no matter how small. Celebrating milestones reinforces the idea that hard work is appreciated. For instance, sending an encouraging note to congratulate a colleague on a successful project strengthens the bonds of camaraderie.

3. Daily Affirmations: Make it a practice to share daily affirmations within your circle. Each day, encourage others by expressing one positive trait or achievement you admire about them. By making this a habit, the atmosphere transforms into one of constant encouragement.

Scriptural Foundations of Encouragement

The Bible is rich with teachings that highlight the importance of encouragement in communication. As believers, we can draw inspiration from various passages that showcase God's intent for our words.

- Hebrews 10:24-25 reminds us, 'And let us consider how to stir up one another to love and good works, not neglecting to meet together…' This verse emphasises the responsibility of believers to encourage and uplift one another actively.
- 1 Thessalonians 5:11 implores us, 'Therefore encourage one another and build one another up, just as you are doing.' This command highlights the importance of continual encouragement in our relationships.

Fostering an understanding of these principles can deepen our commitment to nurturing positive dialogue. By grounding our conversations in scripture, we align our intentions with God's vision for loving communication.

Navigating Difficult Conversations with Grace

Nurturing positive dialogue also extends to challenging discussions. There may be moments when maintaining an uplifting tone feels challenging, yet even in these instances, the principles of encouragement can guide us.

Consider these tips when navigating tough conversations:

1. Stay Centred in Grace: Approach difficult conversations with a grace-centred mindset. This means prioritising understanding over being right, focusing on building bridges rather than walls.

2. Use 'I' Statements: Communicate your feelings and thoughts without assigning blame. Instead of saying, 'You always dismiss my ideas,' try, 'I feel overlooked when my input isn't acknowledged.' This technique fosters constructive dialogue without inciting defensiveness.

3. Seek Common Ground: During disputes, emphasise shared values and goals. By recognising mutual aspirations, you can create a foundation for encouragement even amidst disagreement.

4. Follow Up: After a challenging conversation, revisit the topic later to affirm your intentions and express appreciation for the person's willingness to engage. A simple, 'Thank you for discussing that with me. I value your perspective,' goes a long way in nurturing relationships.

The Long-Term Impact of Uplifting Speech

The cumulative effect of nurturing positive dialogue can profoundly influence the trajectory of our relationships. Words expressed in kindness often create ripples that can extend far beyond immediate exchanges, impacting not only those directly involved but also their communities.

Research backs the notion that positive speech promotes psychological well-being. Individuals who regularly engage in uplifting dialogue report higher levels of satisfaction in their relationships, improved mental health outcomes, and greater resilience to stress. Thus, each act of encouragement can serve as a strategic investment in the emotional infrastructure of our lives.

Transforming Challenging Relationships

Furthermore, uplifting speech can breathe new life into challenging relationships. By breaking the cycle of negative dialogue, individuals can shift the narrative, paving the way for healing and reconciliation. Acts of kindness and support can redefine perceptions and transform adversarial relationships into positive alliances.

Consider the story of Joseph in Genesis. Despite the adversity and betrayal from his brothers, his journey ultimately led to reconciliation and restoration. Joseph chose to respond with grace and forgiveness, illustrating the profound power of encouraging words in addressing even the deepest wounds.

Practical Exercises to Cultivate Positive Dialogue

To cement these principles into everyday practice, engage in the following practical exercises that will help ingrain the art of uplifting speech into your daily life:

1. Daily Affirmation Journal: Start each day by writing down three positive affirmations for yourself and three for someone else. This practice encourages you to consciously seek out positivity in your life and the lives of others.

2. Encouragement Challenge: Commit to sharing a word of encouragement daily for a week. This can be achieved through a text, email, or handwritten note—a small gesture can have a significant impact.

3. Reflection Time: Set aside moments for reflection after conversations. Consider what was said and how it could have been presented in a more uplifting manner. This practice fosters growth and deepens self-awareness.

4. Role Reversal: When in dialogue with someone, practice expressing their words back to them in an encouraging manner. This helps you recognise their perspective and reinforces their voice, nurturing a deeper connection.

The Ripple Effect of Positive Dialogue

As we nurture positive dialogue in our lives, we create a ripple effect. Every encouraging conversation can spark a chain reaction, inspiring others to contribute kindness and support in their own interactions. This web of positivity woven through speech has the potential to inspire and uplift entire communities, extending beyond our immediate circle into the world around us.

Effects of Nurturing Positive Dialogue

In nurturing positive dialogue, we embrace profound biblical truths while cultivating our relationships with intention and hope. Encouragement is not merely a nicety; it is an essential practice that can profoundly transform hearts, minds, and connections. As we commit to upholding a culture of uplifting speech, we align ourselves with God's design for communication, where every word we speak becomes a seed of light, capable of blossoming into something beautiful.

Reflect on how you can actively nurture positive dialogue in your conversations. The time is always right to start sowing seeds of encouragement and positivity, creating vibrant gardens of connection and trust in the lives of those around you.

Tending to Weeds of Doubt

In every garden, we find the potential for beauty, growth, and abundance. Yet alongside the vibrant blooms and budding fruits, there lurk unwanted intruders—weeds that can stifle growth and drain the nutrients from the soil. Just as a gardener must diligently tend to their plants, so too must we care for the words we speak and the thoughts we entertain. In this subchapter, we will explore the significance of addressing the weeds of doubt within our speech and thoughts. By uprooting negativity and cultivating a space for faith-filled affirmations, we can foster an environment that nurtures healthy, constructive dialogue.

Identifying Negative Speech Patterns

The journey toward cultivating enriching conversations begins with self-awareness. Our minds are often perpetually busy, and within that noise lie thoughts that can sabotage our ability to communicate effectively. Before we can address these patterns, we first have to recognise them.

Negative speech patterns manifest in various forms. Perhaps we find ourselves engaging in self-deprecating remarks, criticising others unnecessarily, or communicating in ways that amplify cynicism and doubt. These detrimental expressions not only hinder our relationships but also reflect our inner struggles, often revealing insecurities that need to be addressed.

A useful exercise to help identify these patterns is to maintain a journal for a week. Each day, take a few moments to reflect on your conversations—both those you initiated and those that occurred around you. How did you engage with others? Did you uplift or demoralise? Record specific instances where you noticed negativity seep into your speech. As you do this, pay attention not only to your words but also to the emotions attached to them. Were you feeling anxious, defensive, or pessimistic? By becoming attuned to these emotions, you can start to connect them with specific thought patterns.

It's essential to understand the underlying beliefs that feed negative speech. Often, our words act as a reflection of our self-image and our perception of the world around us. For instance, if you frequently express mistrust in others, it's likely rooted in personal experiences of disappointment or betrayal. Likewise, a tendency to critique rather than encourage may come from internalised fears about your worthiness or abilities. Once you've identified these destructive patterns and their origins, you can begin to address them systematically.

Uprooting Doubt and Cynicism

Having identified negative speech patterns, the next step is to actively uproot these weeds of doubt and cynicism. This process requires mindfulness, intention, and a commitment to transformation.

1. Challenge Doubt with Truth

Begin by identifying specific phrases or thoughts that you recognise as perpetuating doubt. These might sound like: 'I'll never succeed,' 'What's the point?' or 'People let me down.' Once you've identified these beliefs, challenge their validity. Ask yourself questions like: What evidence backs these assertions? How have I succeeded despite past difficulties? Are there instances that prove these thoughts to be untrue?

Replacing these negative thoughts with truth is essential. Affirmations rooted in faith can serve as effective replacements. They not only counteract doubt but also nourish our spirits. For instance, instead of saying, 'I can't do this,' you might replace it with 'Through Christ, I am capable of all things.' Regularly practising such affirmations can rewire your thought processes, encouraging a more positive outlook.

2. Practice Gratitude

Gratitude is a powerful antidote to doubt and cynicism. When you cultivate a habit of gratitude, you shift your focus from what's lacking to what you already have. Each day, take some time to list three things you're grateful for, both big and small. This could range from a warm cup of coffee in the morning to the support of a friend during a tough time.

As you practice gratitude, you create a mental environment that fosters positivity. When speaking with others, aim to include expressions of gratitude in your conversations. Instead of focusing on complaints or negatives, emphasise appreciation for the people and experiences in your life. This shift not only enriches your own life but can also cultivate a more uplifting atmosphere in your interactions.

3. Surround Yourself with Positivity

The company we keep has a profound impact on our speech and thought patterns. Make a conscious effort to surround yourself with positive influences—people who foster encouragement and uplift your spirit. Seek out friends, mentors, or faith communities that reflect the values you desire to embody.

Engaging with uplifting material, whether through books, podcasts, or sermons, can also reinforce positive speech. These sources provide insight into the power of words and encourage a faith-filled perspective on challenges. When you fill your mind with positive messages, you are less likely to succumb to negativity in your speech.

4. Engage in Constructive Conversations

When faced with situations that typically lead to negative speech, prepare to engage in more constructive conversations. Consider framing your dialogues with curiosity and openness instead of judgment. For example, if you feel the urge to criticise, ask open-ended questions that invite understanding: 'What challenges did you face?' or 'How did that experience shape your perspective?' This shift in approach not only showcases empathy but also fosters a mutual exploration of ideas and perspectives.

It's often through authentic conversations that we can replace cynicism with hope. By engaging with others honestly and compassionately, we can collectively focus on finding solutions rather than dwelling on problems. Look for opportunities in every conversation to build up rather than tear down. Shift your language from one of defeat to one of potential and possibility.

5. Set Intentions for Your Speech

One of the most powerful acts we can undertake is to set daily intentions for our speech. Each morning, take a moment to pray or reflect, seeking divine guidance on how to communicate in a way that embodies love and faith. These intentions could be as simple as, 'Today, I will be mindful of my words,' or 'I will seek opportunities to encourage others.'

By setting such intentions, you create a framework for your interactions. When doubts or negative thoughts arise during your day, refer back to your intentions as a reminder of the positive impact you wish to have on those around you.

Replacing Negativity with Faith-Filled Affirmations

Having uprooted doubt and negativity, the next principal action is to cultivate an atmosphere of faith-filled affirmations. This process involves actively integrating positive and faith-based statements into your daily communication.

1. Develop a Personal Affirmation List

Start by creating a personalised list of affirmations that resonate with your faith and aspirations. These should reflect your reliance on God's promises and your belief in your potential. For instance:

- I am loved unconditionally by God.
- I am capable of achieving great things through Christ.
- My words have the power to heal and uplift.

Once you've compiled your list, make it a habit to read these affirmations aloud daily. Reciting them provides a meaningful ritual that strengthens your commitment to positive dialogue.

2. Incorporate Affirmations into Conversations

As you interact with others, be intentional in weaving your affirmations into your language. Use phrases like 'I believe we can find a solution together' or 'I trust in the goodness that surrounds us.' Such affirmations not only influence your mindset but also encourage those around you. You create an atmosphere filled with hope, inspiring others to embrace positivity and faith through your words.

3. Model Affirmative Language

It's important to serve as a model for language that cultivates faith and positivity. Approach conversations with a mindset that affirms others' strengths and potential. Recognise achievements, however small, and express appreciation for efforts made, often going unnoticed.

Words such as 'I appreciate your hard work' or 'Your contributions truly matter' serve as affirmations that fortify others, creating a ripple effect of positivity.

4. Practice Forgiveness

A significant component of cultivating faith-filled dialogue involves forgiveness, both towards yourself and others. Past conversations may be littered with doubts, negativity, or harsh words. Allow yourself grace for these moments and recognise them as opportunities for growth.

Additionally, be open to forgiving others for any hurtful words they've spoken towards you. When you release these burdens, you free yourself from the weight of resentment and make space for constructive communication.

5. Join a Supportive Community

Surrounding yourself with individuals who value positivity and affirming speech can significantly impact your journey. Consider joining a group where discussing and sharing affirmations and encouragement is part of the culture. Whether it's a small church group, a support circle, or a friendship network, engaging with others who emphasise healthy dialogue will reinforce your commitment.

6. Monitor Your Inner Dialogue

Often, our most damaging speech patterns occur within our minds. Pay attention to the way you speak to yourself daily. Are your internal affirmations positive and affirming, or are they harsh critiques?

Make it a practice to shift negative self-talk into constructive affirmations. If you catch yourself thinking, 'I can't believe I said that,' reframe it as, 'I am learning and growing from this experience.' Over time, nurturing a positive inner dialogue will enhance your confidence and ability to communicate effectively.

Cultivating Healthy and Fruitful Dialogue

Through uprooting doubt and embracing faith-filled affirmations, we cultivate an enriching landscape for meaningful relationships and impactful conversations. This nurturing process involves continuous engagement, commitment, and grace as we strive to speak life into our interactions.

As you practice these techniques, take notice of the gradual shifts in your conversations and relationships. Healthy speech nurtures connections, fostering an environment of love and support.

1. Embrace Active Listening

Beyond what you say, how you listen proves equally critical in building fruitful dialogue. Active listening involves not just hearing words but also seeking to understand. When engaging in conversations, focus on the speaker, clarify points as needed, and respond thoughtfully.

2. Create Opportunities for Shared Affirmations

In every gathering - whether it's a family dinner, a team meeting, or a community gathering - introduce an intentional time of affirmation. Encourage participants to share something good they see in one another. This practice promotes an atmosphere of appreciation and mutual respect, reinforcing positive speech habits.

3. Reflect on Conversations

After significant interactions, take a moment to reflect on them. Consider what went well and what could improve. This reflection can help you identify areas where you can change your speech patterns and contribute positively in future dialogues.

4. Seek Feedback

Lastly, don't hesitate to seek feedback on how others perceive your speech and communication style. Be open to constructive criticism and use it as a tool for growth. Feedback is a gift that can propel your growth and enhance your ability to encourage and uplift others.

In conclusion, addressing the weeds of doubt in our speech is critical to cultivating a garden of life-affirming dialogue. By identifying negative patterns, replacing them with faith-filled affirmations, and committing to supportive communication practices, we nurture healthier and more fruitful interactions. Remember, the words we plant today will undoubtedly shape the gardens of tomorrow—so let's tend them with care, faith, and love.

Amplified Echoes: Shaping Identity Through Words

Colouring Our Narratives

Language is not merely a tool for communication; it is the very brush that paints the canvas of our identity. Every word we utter contributes to the story we tell about ourselves, creating narratives that can either shine brightly with colours of confidence and hope or fade into the background, dull and muted. In this subchapter, we delve into the intricate relationship between language and identity, examining how our choice of words not only shapes our self-perception but also influences how others perceive us.

To understand the power of language in shaping identity, we must first acknowledge that our words carry an immense weight. Language serves as a reflection of our thoughts, feelings, and beliefs. When we speak, we unconsciously choose words that align with our internal narratives. This is not a mere coincidence; it speaks to the relationship between our self-perception and the vocabulary at our disposal.

Consider the difference between saying, 'I am struggling' versus 'I am learning.' The former paints a picture of defeat and helplessness, while the latter reflects growth and resilience. Each phrase offers a different lens through which to view an experience. Choosing the right words has the potential to enhance our self-image, turning challenging situations into opportunities for growth. Our language can elevate our stories, allowing us to frame our identity in a way that reflects our aspirations and dreams.

Our narratives are constantly being crafted and reshaped by the words we use. In a world where social media and instant communication dominate, the words we choose can construct our public personas, influencing how others perceive us and how we perceive ourselves. The digital age has further amplified the significance of our language; the stories we tell online can become integral parts of our identity. In crafting our online profiles and statuses, we often curate a narrative designed to impress, resonate, and connect with others. However, this curated persona can lead to dissonance if it diverges from our authentic selves. The gap between our true voices and our public narratives can sow seeds of confusion, leading to feelings of isolation or inadequacy when faced with the disparity.

Words possess the power to create vibrant stories filled with passion and purpose, or they can yield muted tales, lacking the authenticity and vibrancy that give them life. The essential question becomes: what kind of narrative are we creating through our language? Are we crafting an inspiring story that aligns with our faith, values, and aspirations, or are we allowing doubt and negativity to seep into our dialogue, inadvertently dulling the vibrancy of our identity?

To explore the colours of our narratives further, it is crucial to engage in self-reflection. Self-reflection is the practice of looking inward to examine our thoughts, beliefs, and motivations. When we reflect on how our words shape our identity, we can gain deeper insights into ourselves. This process encourages us to ask vital questions about the language we use daily: Are our words affirming or critical? Do they strengthen our identity or undermine it?

For instance, if you often catch yourself using words that diminish your worth—such as 'I'm not good enough' or 'I never succeed'—it is time to acknowledge that these words create a muted narrative. In contrast, reframing these statements as 'I am capable' and 'I am continuously improving' can allow your identity to blossom into something vibrant.

We can challenge ourselves to examine the language we employ, not just in self-talk but also in our interactions with others. Words spoken in conversations with friends, family, and colleagues offer insight into how we perceive our surroundings and ourselves.

Do we engage in discussions that uplift us, or do we find ourselves trapped in exchanges that diminish our spirits?

Let us take a closer look at the dynamics of these interactions. When we engage in a conversation filled with negative language, we not only echo that negativity in our words but also within our hearts. Consider the impact of uttering phrases like 'I hate my job,' 'People are so untrustworthy,' or 'Everything always goes wrong for me.' Over time, such language dulls our spirit and colours our identity with despair and frustration.

In contrast, engaging in dialogues filled with affirmation and enthusiasm paints a vastly different picture. By saying, 'I'm grateful for the challenges that help me grow,' or 'I enjoy connecting with genuine people,' we foster an environment in which our identity can flourish. Our words then become a reflection of the vibrant individual we aspire to be.

The connection between language and identity is reinforced through communal interactions as well. In fellowship with others, we share narratives that intertwine with their own. The stories we tell and the words we choose become collective threads that bind us together in community. Each narrative contributes to a larger tapestry, illustrating the interconnectedness of our lives.

The Power of Words

Just as a painter mixes colours to achieve depth and dimension, we can combine our personal narratives with the experiences and insights of others to enrich our identities. In moments of listening and sharing our stories, we create a space for growth and transformation. We learn from one another, allowing our language and ideas to coalesce into a richer understanding of who we are and who we aspire to become.

To cultivate this reflection, consider establishing a journaling practice. Write about your daily conversations, noting the language that resonated with you positively or negatively. Reflect on how your words have influenced your emotions and interactions. This practice not only enhances self-awareness but also enables you to identify patterns in your language that may require change.

Our identities are not just formed by the words we speak, but also by the stories we tell ourselves about our feelings and experiences. These narratives often encompass the broader themes of our lives—success, failure, joy, and sorrow. The self-talk we engage in can either empower us or imprison us within limiting beliefs. The challenge is to recognise when our self-narratives become detrimental and to reshape them into stories of resilience and hope.

This reshaping process resembles that of reworking a piece of art. Just as an artist can add layers, remove excess, or redefine the structure to align with a vision, we too can revise our narratives. By consciously choosing language that empowers, embraces hope, and reflects our faith, we can transform the stories we tell ourselves into powerful affirmations of identity.

Therefore, self-accountability becomes crucial in this journey towards crafting a vibrant narrative. It is not enough to simply recognise the power of words; we must actively engage in practices that encourage us to use language that uplifts ourselves and those around us. This level of accountability requires us to monitor both our internal dialogues and our external conversations. It demands honesty and a willingness to challenge negative thought patterns or spoken words.

Faith plays a central role in this endeavour. As we align our language with the teachings of our faith, we begin to see how divinely inspired words can breathe life into our narratives. Scriptural guidance offers us a wellspring of affirmations and truths that can shape how we communicate with ourselves and others.

For instance, the Bible teaches about the power of words in Proverbs 18:21, where it is written: 'The tongue has the power of life and death, and those who love it will eat its fruit.' This powerful verse encapsulates the notion that our words can either nourish or destroy, a concept that resonates deeply with our journey of identity formation. When we accept this truth, we find motivation to choose words that create life—uplifting words that reflect our faith, values, and aspirations.

As we delve deeper into the art of colouring our narratives, we will also explore the significance of storytelling as a means of creating meaning. Sharing our stories—whether through personal testimony, creative expression, or communal sharing—invites reflections of our authentic selves into the light. The act of narrating our experiences reinforces the notion that our stories matter, and they are integral to the identities we construct.

We must illuminate our personal experiences with vulnerability. Allowing others to see our authentic selves fosters connection and empathy, urging counterparts to engage in their self-reflection. Sharing our struggles or triumphs can create a space for dialogue and healing. Such exchanges remind us that we are not alone in our narratives; we are woven into a community where words can connect hearts and minds.

Just as a story can inspire, it can also challenge the listener to reflect on their narratives. The challenge becomes a tool for growth, illuminating the areas within our identities that may require transformation. For example, when we hear stories of triumph in the face of adversity, our perspectives may shift. We might begin to see our struggles as opportunities for growth rather than insurmountable obstacles.

Through the lenses of others, we can also reshape the narratives we tell ourselves. A simple shift from an outsider's perspective can often lead to a breakthrough in self-understanding. The very act of active listening allows us to step outside of ourselves and gain insights that enrich our identities.

In recognising the multifaceted dimensions of our stories, we also acknowledge the presence of external narratives that influence our identities. Societal expectations, cultural backgrounds, and familial legacies can all contribute to the stories we tell about ourselves. While some of these narratives may empower us, others can constrict and diminish our sense of self. The challenge lies in discerning which influences are beneficial and which need addressing or reframing.

To foster a vibrant narrative, we must take a stand against limiting beliefs imposed by societal or cultural norms. This calls for courage—a willingness to challenge the narratives that do not serve us. As we embrace the unique story of our lives, we find strength in authenticity, realising that our experiences are valid and worthy of being expressed. In doing so, we liberate ourselves from the constraints of others' expectations and reclaim the vibrant hues of our identity.

Resilience becomes key in this journey—resilience to affirm one's identity amidst challenges and to use language that reflects the inherent value we hold. When negative external narratives threaten to dull our colours, we can respond with an unwavering declaration of possibility. We can reaffirm, 'I am gifted,' 'I am worthy,' 'I am capable.'

In conclusion, the subchapter 'Colouring Our Narratives' invites us to embark on a transformative journey of self-discovery through the words we choose. As we reflect on how language shapes our identity, we recognise our agency in crafting meaningful narratives that resonate with our core values. The power of language is profound; every word is a stroke on the canvas of our identity. Let us choose wisely, boldly, and brightly, colouring our stories with the vibrant hues of hope, faith, and love.

The Power of Affirmation

Words hold incredible power—they can shape our identities and influence our experiences. Particularly, the words we use in affirmations can serve as a beacon of light, illuminating our paths and fortifying our self-esteem. In this subchapter, we will explore

The Power of Words

the profound impact that positive affirmations can have, not only on those around us but also on our self-perception. By incorporating affirmations into our daily conversations, we can cultivate a positive environment that fosters growth, confidence, and resilience.

Affirmations, at their core, are positive statements that influence our thoughts and attitudes. When spoken with intention and belief, they reinforce positive self-images and foster a climate of encouragement, whether directed towards ourselves or others. By understanding the significance of affirmations, we will unlock the incredible potential they hold to shape our realities.

To grasp the power of affirmations, we must first recognise the essential role that words play in our lives. Our identities are deeply intertwined with the language we use. Language not only allows us to express our thoughts and feelings, but it also helps shape our mindset. The words we choose to define ourselves can either build us up or tear us down. Consequently, this subchapter's exploration of affirmations will reveal how intentionally choosing positive language can elevate our self-identity.

Consider this: when we speak positive words of affirmation, we engage in a transformative act. Words such as 'I am capable,' 'I am loved,' or 'I am enough' resonate deeply within us, working to reshape our beliefs about ourselves. These phrases serve as powerful reminders of our inherent value, gently nudging us towards self-acceptance. The practice of affirmations can create a domino effect in our lives, enabling not just individual growth but also the ability to uplift others. As we affirm ourselves, we become agents of positivity in the lives of those we encounter, fostering relationships characterised by support and encouragement.

The roots of affirmations can be traced back to various ancient teachings, including biblical principles. In the Scriptures, we find numerous passages that proclaim the significance of words. Proverbs 18:21 states, 'The tongue has the power of life and death, and those who love it will eat its fruit.' This powerful verse serves as a stern reminder that our words have consequences, capable of bringing about empowering change or, conversely, deep harm. Therefore, as believers, we are called to speak life into our surroundings, utilising affirmations to create a positive atmosphere rooted in love.

To effectively harness the power of affirmations, we must first cultivate an understanding of their structure. A well-articulated affirmation typically contains three essential components: positivity, present-tense language, and personal ownership. It's more than just stating something you would like to be true; it's about claiming your truth as if it were already reality. Instead of saying, 'I want to be confident,' a more potent affirmation would be, 'I am confident.' The latter carries an air of certainty and belief that the subconscious can grapple with and start to manifest in our daily lives.

In addition to the structure of affirmations, the consistent practice of affirming ourselves can transform our thoughts over time. Many people struggle with negative self-talk—a cycle that can be challenging to break free from. Affirmations serve as an antidote to that negativity, providing a structured way to confront and redirect harmful thoughts. This change doesn't occur overnight, but with commitment and repetition, affirmations can reshape our internal dialogues and foster resilience against doubt and fear.

As we delve deeper into the importance of affirmations, it is essential to consider the impact they can have not only on ourselves but also on those around us. Think about a time when someone affirmed you; perhaps a friend praised your new idea, or a loved one reminded you of your strengths during tough times. Those words likely empowered you to embrace your potential and pursue your goals with renewed energy. Just as one positive interaction can create an uplifting experience, consistently affirming others can strengthen connections and deepen relationships.

The principle of affirming others aligns with the biblical teaching found in 1 Thessalonians 5:11, which encourages us to 'encourage one another and build each other up.' When we speak affirming words to others, we can positively influence their perception of themselves, reinforcing their worth. As we create an environment filled with encouragement, we cultivate trust, connection, and cooperation—elements essential for healthy and thriving relationships. This ripple effect highlights the synergistic nature of affirmation. As we build each other up, we encourage a culture of support, facilitating growth for both individuals and communities.

Incorporating affirmations into our daily lives doesn't require grand gestures; even small, simple phrases can initiate change. By expressing appreciation for a friend or acknowledging the efforts of a team member, you send ripples of positivity that can uplift spirits and boost morale. Regularly practising affirmations—whether by keeping a gratitude journal, verbalising your strengths in front of a mirror, or sending encouraging texts—can transform the way we perceive ourselves and resonate within our relationships.

To set ourselves up for success with affirmations, it can be helpful to create a routine. Set aside time each day to reflect on your affirmations: say them aloud, write them down, and visualise them manifesting in your life. Morning affirmations can set a purposeful tone for your day, giving you the assurance you need to face challenges. Evening reflections can serve to ground you, reinforcing a sense of accomplishment as you note how your day aligned with your stated affirmations.

As we consider various techniques for incorporating affirmations into our lives, it becomes vital to establish a repertoire tailored to our individual needs. Personalisation is key. The most effective affirmations resonate with your specific circumstances, goals, and aspirations. Create affirmations that scribe the narrative you desire, articulating your visions for the future and your ongoing journey of self-discovery.

Combining visual aids can also enhance the power of affirmations. Some individuals find it helpful to create vision boards that encapsulate their goals and aspirations. Images can accompany your written affirmations, providing a sense of clarity and purpose. Surrounding yourself with reminders of your affirmations—whether in the form of sticky notes, motivational quotes, or visual imagery—can reinforce your commitment to positive self-talk and allow for constant inspiration.

Another avenue for manifesting affirmations is through the practice of prayer. For individuals of faith, incorporating affirmations with worship can foster a profound spiritual connection. Seek divine support by aligning your affirmations with Scripture. When you affirm your strengths and potential, pray for guidance and strength to live those words out authentically. This practice enriches the experience of affirmations by placing them in the context of faith, allowing you to draw on spiritual resources as you affirm your identity.

It is essential to acknowledge that affirmations are not a cure-all. Life's complexities can often lead to feelings of doubt and inadequacy, even in the face of consistent positive reinforcement. External factors, such as criticism, failure, or unrealistic societal expectations, can undermine our confidence, making it imperative to pair affirmations with self-compassion.

Self-compassion nurtures a gentle approach to our flaws and failures. It acknowledges that we are human, capable of growth, yet imperfect. Instead of berating ourselves for perceived shortcomings, we can offer the same kindness we would extend to a friend. Affirmations can stand in harmony with self-compassion, reminding us that while we strive for improvement, we are still inherently deserving of love and acceptance.

As we delve further into the intricacies of affirmations, we must reflect on the cumulative impact of these affirmations over time. Like seeds sown in fertile soil, affirmations require patience and nurturing to bear fruit. Sometimes the fruits of our labour can take longer to manifest than we anticipate. However, the unwavering commitment to affirming ourselves and others will gradually lead to a shift in our perceptions, relationships, and overall well-being.

Consider constructing a cycle of affirmation in your life. Begin with small seeds of positivity and build upon them with consistent practice. This could mean acknowledging daily successes, celebrating milestones, and encouraging others as they navigate their journeys. As you cultivate this cycle, you'll witness growth not only in your identity but also in your community—nurturing an environment resonant with encouragement, hope, and motivation.

The evidence supporting the efficacy of affirmations is grounded in psychological research and the practices of numerous individuals across cultures and backgrounds. Individuals who actively engage in affirmations tend to report higher levels of self-esteem and overall well-being. Scientific studies have shown that positive self-affirmations can counteract the effects of stress and anxiety, leading to improved mental health outcomes.

In conclusion, affirmations are not mere words strung together; they are powerful tools capable of carving our self-images and influencing our interactions. By incorporating affirmations into our daily conversations, we can foster meaningful dialogues that uplift ourselves and those around us. The journey of cultivating positive affirmations is indeed transformative, allowing us to amplify echoes of encouragement and shape our identities in alignment with our true potential. As we adopt this practice, we are reminded that our words—whether spoken, written, or thought—hold the power of life and death. Let us wield this power wisely, uplifting ourselves and others through the beautiful gift of affirmation.

Narratives of Transformation

As we journey through life, we often overlook the profound impact our words have not only on those around us but also on ourselves. The narratives that shape our identities are deeply intertwined with the language we choose to express our experiences, feelings, and beliefs. In this final subsection, we will delve into profound stories that reflect individual transformations triggered by the conscious choice of words and mindful speech. These stories serve as a testament to the potential for change that lies within each of us when we harness the power of language.

Our first narrative takes us into the life of Samuel, a young man whose journey of self-discovery began in a challenging environment. Growing up in a neighbourhood that often celebrated negativity, Samuel found himself trapped in a cycle of self-doubt and despair. His interactions were riddled with sarcasm and bitterness, mirroring the words that echoed around him daily.

However, everything changed when he attended a weekend retreat focused on the power of words.

During this retreat, Samuel engaged in deep conversations and reflective exercises that emphasised the importance of uplifting language. He learned about the transformative nature of his speech, realising that the words he chose were a direct reflection of his thoughts and self-perception. Inspired by this revelation, Samuel adopted a new approach to both his internal dialogue and conversations with others. Every morning, he began writing down positive affirmations—simple yet powerful phrases, such as 'I am worthy' and 'I can overcome challenges.'

Gradually, the shift in Samuel's language began to affect his identity. His newfound commitment to mindful speech not only altered how he viewed himself but also changed how others perceived him. Friends and family noticed his transformation, noting his increased positivity and willingness to support others. Samuel's journey exemplifies how a commitment to uplifting speech can ignite a radical transformation, paving the way for self-love and growth.

Next, we explore the story of Maria, a middle-aged woman who found herself weighed down by her past. Having faced years of criticism from peers and loved ones, Maria internalised their negative comments, which stifled her self-esteem. For years, she uttered self-deprecating remarks, reinforcing her feelings of inadequacy. It wasn't until she joined a community of women focused on empowerment that Maria discovered the transformative effect of supportive dialogue.

In this nurturing environment, Maria was encouraged to share her experiences openly. Listening to stories of other women who had overcome similar struggles inspired her to reflect on her speech patterns. She actively worked to replace her limiting beliefs with affirmations that celebrated her strengths and achievements. The power of kind words wasn't just external to her but also began reshaping how she viewed herself. When she would feel tempted to belittle her accomplishments, she would counter those thoughts with phrases like 'I am enough' and 'I have unique talents.'

Maria's narrative illustrates that the practice of transforming language can lead to inner healing. With every kind word she spoke—both to herself and others—she opened doors to self-acceptance, confidence, and ultimately, compassion. She even began hosting workshops in her community, helping others understand how intentional language could uplift and empower them.

The Power of Words

Equally powerful is the story of David, a high school teacher who realised the influence he had on his students' lives through his words. Initially, David's teaching style was traditional, sticking closely to the curriculum without allowing much room for emotional engagement. Over time, however, he noticed that many of his students struggled with confidence and self-worth, often retreating into silence rather than actively participating in class.

Motivated to shift this dynamic, David began implementing mindful communication in his teaching. He introduced practices such as morning affirmations and positive reinforcement, encouraging his students to articulate their thoughts without fear of judgment. He shared his struggles with self-doubt, demonstrating vulnerability that allowed students to relate to him on a human level.

As David's classroom transformed into a safe space for emotional expression, he witnessed remarkable changes. Students who once sat quietly in the back began to share their thoughts, contribute to discussions, and engage with the material in new and more active ways. Through simple yet profound conversations, David cultivated a culture of support and encouragement, ultimately helping his students recognise their unique gifts and strengths.

David's story underscores the ripple effect that mindful speech can have, extending beyond the individual to cultivate a supportive community. Words possess the power to heal, inspire, and transform not just the speaker but also those who listen.

Maria and David's narratives beautifully demonstrate how language shapes identity, but let's not overlook Liz, a businesswoman whose transformation began in the boardroom. For years, Liz felt the weight of imposter syndrome, feeling unworthy of leadership despite her achievements. Facing a critical client meeting, she often succumbed to feelings of inadequacy, opting for meek language that undermined her position.

Seeking guidance from a mentor, Liz learned about the concept of 'power posing'—an exercise that emphasises physical postures in conjunction with confident language. Inspired by the research on the psychological benefits of empowered body language, she decided to step out of her comfort zone. Liz committed to adopting powerful words that embodied her expertise and confidence during presentations.

As she embraced this change, Liz noticed a significant transformation not only in her professional demeanour but also in her relationships with colleagues. By asserting herself and using affirmative language, she began to command respect and leadership. The trust and admiration she cultivated accelerated her career, culminating in a promotion to a senior position. Liz's experience illustrates how shifting our language in professional settings can redefine our roles and perceptions.

Additionally, we cannot overlook the story of Rashid, a young man from a diverse background who struggled with his identity and sense of belonging. Growing up between two cultures, he often felt the pressure to choose one identity over another. This inner conflict manifested in self-doubt, evident in the way he communicated with others. Rashid often downplayed his achievements and hesitated to express his heritage, fearing judgment or misunderstanding.

Through a program focused on cultural dialogue, Rashid discovered the power of storytelling as a means of connection. He learned how to share his experiences in a way that celebrated both sides of his identity, framing his narrative in a context that honoured the richness of diversity. Embracing this newfound ability, he began to articulate his journey confidently, challenging misconceptions and fostering appreciation for his background among his peers.

Rashid's story highlights the vital role of language in navigating complex identities. When we choose to share our narratives without shame or fear, we create opportunities for connection and mutual understanding, fostering a richer, more inclusive dialogue.

As we reflect upon these powerful narratives, it's essential to recognise that the journey of transformation through mindful speech is not merely anecdotal—it is profoundly rooted in the biblical principles that encourage us to harness the potency of words. The Scriptures remind us in Proverbs 18:21 that 'The tongue has the power of life and death, and those who love it will eat its fruit.' This ancient wisdom affirms the notion that our words hold the capability to shape not only our lives but also the lives of those around us.

Moreover, mindful communication requires intentional practice and a willingness to embrace vulnerability. Each individual's journey is unique, but the principles of love, respect, and authenticity resonate universally. As we encourage one another to adopt a language of compassion and kindness, we can collectively create an environment where growth and transformation flourish.

In closing, the narratives shared here serve as beacons of hope and inspiration. They remind us that our words can either bind us or set us free. When we choose to engage with language that uplifts, enlightens, and empowers, we release the potential for profound transformation within ourselves and our communities. Each testimony illustrates the capacity for change that resides within every individual, emphasising that the journey toward mindful speech is a pathway to understanding, healing, and connection.

As you reflect on these stories, consider your narratives. How have your words shaped your life? What transformations are waiting to unfold as you commit to embracing the power of mindful speech? Let these tales inspire you to speak with intention, nurture your relationships, and tap into the endless possibilities that arise when we harness the divine power of language.

Your journey toward transformation, empowered by the power of words, begins today. Take the steps to amplify your voice, shape your identity, and make a positive impact on the world around you.

Tidal Waves or Gentle Breezes? The Impact of Our Conversations

The Forces of Dialogue

In the vast ocean of human interaction, our words can function with remarkable power, akin to the forces of nature. Just as ocean tides ebb and flow, so too do our conversations possess the potential to surge dramatically or to flow gently. Understanding this comparison illuminates the impact of our communication and helps us recognise how the way we speak shapes our relationships and the emotional landscape of those around us.

The ocean itself serves as a perfect metaphor for dialogue. At times, it is calm—waves barely lapping at the shore. In those moments, conversations can feel easy. Other times, the ocean is turbulent, with waves crashing against the rocks, symbolising discussions that are fraught with emotion, conflict, and unpredictability. Each interaction we have carries the potential to either create a harmonious symphony or unleash a formidable storm.

Consider how a casual conversation may resemble gentle waves lapping at a beach. In these moments, the dialogue flows effortlessly, much like a soothing whisper that brings tranquillity to

The Power of Words

our interactions. This kind of communication fosters connection, nurturing a bond that can gradually strengthen over time. It's the exchange of pleasant pleasantries among friends or family, the shared laughter, and the light-hearted discussions that add warmth to our relationships. In these gentle breezes of conversation, we find opportunities to express our shared values and beliefs, reinforcing the fabric of our connections.

Conversely, it's crucial to acknowledge the potential for dialogue to turn tumultuous—a tide capable of sweeping away the cherished connections we've nurtured. Conversations can ignite feelings of anger, frustration, or defensiveness, leaving emotional debris in their wake. Just as stormy waters can erase the footprints left upon the beach, harsh words can erase the trust and intimacy built up over time. The patterns of speech we choose, whether conscious or unconscious, can leave lasting impressions on our relationships. As we navigate the tumultuous waters of our discourse, it becomes essential to refine our ability to communicate with intention and compassion.

These dualities of dialogue—the tranquil breezes and the fierce tides—invite us to explore key aspects which comprise the forces at play in our interactions. Emotional undercurrents, personal histories, and societal dynamics all swirl beneath the surface of our spoken words, influencing the direction and impact of our conversations.

The Power of Words

We must delve deeper into these elements to understand how they shape our communication styles and affect the emotional climate within our connections.

One fundamental aspect to consider is emotional undercurrents. Just as ocean currents can shift direction, guiding surface waves, our emotions can cloud or clarify our words. When we communicate, we often carry with us an emotional depth that can sway how our message is received. For instance, consider two friends discussing a recent disagreement. If one friend is still harbouring feelings of hurt, their words may emerge with an edge of defensiveness or resentment. In this scenario, what could have been a constructive dialogue instead gives rise to a tidal wave of misunderstandings.

It is vital to recognise these emotional currents—not only within ourselves but also in others. An emotionally charged dialogue requires us to tread carefully, like a sailor navigating rocky waters. Active listening becomes an essential tool, allowing us to gauge the emotional temperature of our conversations. By acknowledging the feelings embedded within our exchanges, we can steer our dialogues toward healing and understanding instead of allowing them to spiral out of control.

Personal histories also heavily influence how our dialogues unfold. Everyone brings a unique set of experiences and backgrounds to the table—like distant shores shaped by countless waves over time. Past traumas, learned behaviours, and formative interactions all play a role in how we choose to communicate. For example, someone who has faced rejection might approach conversations with caution, defensiveness, or even hostility as a means of self-protection. Conversely, someone nurtured in loving environments might engage in dialogue with openness and trust.

These individual histories inform not only the tone of our words but also how we interpret the words of others. In relationships, there exists an undeniable interplay between our histories and those of our conversation partners. Misunderstandings can arise when we superimpose our narratives upon others, leading to tidal clashes when gentle breezes would suffice. To navigate these intricate waters, we must cultivate empathy. Seeking to understand the backgrounds and experiences that shape our conversations enhances our capacity for patience, compassion, and forgiveness.

Sociocultural dynamics also contribute significantly to our conversational landscape. Just as the underlying geological and atmospheric conditions influence the ocean, our words are moulded by the society we inhabit—a swirling mix of norms, expectations, and shared beliefs. For instance, in some cultures, indirect communication is highly valued, and ambiguity can be interpreted as a sign of politeness. In contrast, others prioritise forthrightness, leading to potential conflicts when two differing approaches collide. Cultural nuances often dictate how we express ourselves and what is deemed acceptable in dialogue.

Moreover, social hierarchies and power dynamics can shape the tone and content of conversations, affecting who feels empowered to speak and who feels silenced. In a group setting, those with louder voices or more assertive personalities might monopolise the discussion, while quieter individuals might feel drowned out. This imbalance can foster an environment where only some ideas are heard. Analogous to a storm raging as power and control collide, when one voice dominates, the narrative can become skewed, leading to friction and resentment among those feeling marginalised.

Through this lens, it becomes clear that our conversations demand introspection and self-awareness. Each word we choose carries consequences, rippling through the emotional landscape around us. As we speak, we craft an environment—much like a tide rolling in, bringing along with it the capacity for nourishment, growth, or destruction.

One vital aspect of harnessing the influence of dialogue is learning how to calibrate our communication. Just as sailors adjust their sails to catch the wind, we can change our words and delivery to create the atmosphere we seek in our interactions. Engaging in mindful dialogue involves slowing down and checking in with ourselves and our emotional state before entering discussions. By taking this moment for reflection, we empower ourselves to express our thoughts authentically while remaining grounded in compassion.

For instance, consider the impact of pausing before responding in a conversation—much like allowing the ocean waves to recede before considering one's next move. This moment can serve as a surrogate for emotional regulation, allowing us the space to ask ourselves: What do I want to convey? How might my words be received? How can I ensure that my message fosters understanding rather than discord?

In addition to adjusting our sails, we must remain vigilant to the winds of external influences surrounding our interactions. Just as weather patterns can shape the tide, external factors such as stress, environmental distractions, or shared context can also influence how conversations unfold. Are we fully engaging in the discussion, or are we allowing our attention to be diverted by external stimuli? Being aware of these forces can help us to stay present and grounded in our exchanges, fostering a more apparent connection between ourselves and those with whom we communicate.

The Power of Words

As we learn to adapt our approaches to conversations, we begin to take charge of the outcomes. Embracing the mindset of a mariner, we develop the skills to navigate through the turbulence tossed by storms of misunderstanding and miscommunication. This mastery transforms our words from potential tidal waves of conflict into harmonious breezes, facilitating growth and connection.

Ultimately, the forces of dialogue can serve as either tidal waves or gentle breezes, dramatically impacting the course of our relationships. Each interaction represents an opportunity to cultivate trust, heal wounds, and build bridges of understanding. As we learn to harness our communication with intention, we create an environment where authenticity flourishes—an ocean of possibilities rich with connection and compassion.

As we reflect on the dynamics of dialogue, we must ask ourselves how we can foster greater positivity within our communications. Striving for more transparent and mindful exchanges fosters love, grace, and encouragement. Embracing the gentle breezes of conversational kindness allows us to reflect God's love within our speech, inviting opportunities for deeper engagement in our relationships. By nurturing this awareness and harnessing the forces of dialogue, we can transform our communication into a flowing, life-giving exchange that uplifts both ourselves and those we interact with.

Ultimately, we are tasked with the art of speaking not just words, but the essence of who we are. As we recall the vastness of the ocean, we recognise that our dialogue can either calm storms or create them. By intentionally cultivating dialogue that reflects compassion, understanding, and authenticity, we harness the power of our words to leave a lasting impact that resonates throughout our networks and relationships, much like the eternal ebb and flow of the tides.

Creating Safe Spaces

In our journey through life, we encounter countless conversations that shape our relationships. Some discussions uplift and inspire, while others may cause tension or misunderstanding. The difference often lies not just in the content of our words but in the environment in which those words are exchanged. To foster genuine dialogue, it is essential to create safe spaces where individuals feel comfortable exchanging thoughts and feelings without fear of judgment or reprisal. This chapter explores the elements that contribute to such environments and provides practical strategies for cultivating them in our everyday interactions.

Understanding Safe Spaces

Before we unravel the methods for creating safe spaces, it's crucial to understand what it truly means to have a safe space for conversation. A safe space isn't merely about physical location; it also involves emotional and psychological aspects. It is a nurturing environment where individuals can express themselves authentically, knowing they will be met with empathy and understanding rather than criticism or hostility. Here are some key characteristics that define a safe conversational space:

1. Trust: Trust is the foundation of any safe space. When individuals trust that their feelings and thoughts will be respected, they are more likely to open up and share their thoughts. Building trust takes time and consistent positive interactions.

2. Acceptance: A safe space encourages acceptance—acceptance of diverse perspectives, feelings, and experiences. It involves recognising that everyone's journey is unique and validating their experiences without dismissiveness.

3. Non-judgmental Atmosphere: A crucial element of a safe environment is the absence of judgment. Individuals should feel free to share without worrying about being criticised or ridiculed. This creates an atmosphere of openness.

4. Encouragement: Active encouragement can reinforce the feeling of safety. Words of affirmation and support foster a sense of belonging and motivate individuals to express themselves freely.

5. Empathy: Empathy stands at the forefront of creating safe spaces. When we strive to understand one another's feelings and perspectives, we pave the way for honest and transformational conversations.

Practical Strategies for Creating Safe Spaces

Creating safe spaces for dialogue involves intentional practices and a conscientious approach. Here's a comprehensive guide with practical strategies to nurture these environments:

1. Start with Yourself

Creating safe spaces begins with self-awareness and introspection. As communicators, we must examine our attitudes, biases, and triggers. Here are the steps to take:

- Cultivate Mindfulness: Engage in mindfulness practices that allow you to become aware of your thoughts and emotions. By recognising your feelings and reactions, you can respond more consciously during conversations.
- Check Your Implicit Biases: We all have unconscious biases shaped by our backgrounds and experiences. Take the time to identify these biases, as acknowledging them allows you to engage with others more objectively and respectfully.

- Practice Self-Reflection: Regularly reflect on your communication behaviours. Analyse past conversations, and consider whether your words supported or hindered making a safe space. Ask yourself how you can do better next time.

2. Establish Ground Rules

Setting ground rules creates a framework for dialogue, ensuring everyone understands what is expected. Here are some effective ground rules to consider:

- Confidentiality: Agree that what is shared within the conversation remains private. Knowing that their words will not be shared outside the group encourages openness.
- Respect Personal Boundaries: Allow individuals to set the pace of the conversation. Participants should feel free to share only what they are comfortable discussing, without feeling pressured.
- One Person Speaks at a Time: Encourage a system where only one person talks at a time. This eliminates interruptions and ensures each voice is heard, promoting respect and attentive listening.

- Use 'I' Statements: Encourage participants to convey their thoughts and feelings using 'I' statements. This approach minimises blame and fosters responsibility for personal emotions—a powerful method for expressing feelings without escalating conflict.
- Emphasise Active Listening: Remind everyone of the importance of listening attentively. Foster an understanding that dialogues involve both speaking and listening to each other's experiences.

3. Foster Inclusivity

To create truly safe spaces, we must commit to inclusivity by ensuring that all voices are represented and enriched:

- Invite Diverse Perspectives: Encourage diverse individuals to join conversations. Inclusion not only empowers others but also enriches discussions with varied viewpoints and experiences.
- Validate Experiences: Make an effort to validate others' experiences. When participants share their feelings, affirm their realities and acknowledge their emotions as legitimate.
- Be Mindful of Language: Use language that is inclusive and sensitive to all participants. Being cautious with our

word choices demonstrates respect and consideration for everyone's identity and background.

4. Create a Comfortable Environment

The physical environment can significantly influence the safety of conversations. Consider these elements:

- Choose an Appropriate Setting: Select a quiet and comfortable location for discussions. A calming environment enhances the openness of conversations enough to allow individuals to express their true thoughts.
- Utilise Comfort Items: Allow individuals to bring comfort items or familiar objects to the conversation. This personal touch can alleviate tension and create a sense of security.
- Facilitate Grounding Techniques: Before starting a discussion, engage participants in grounding techniques, such as deep breathing or stretching, to help manage anxiety and create a more tranquil atmosphere.

5. Encourage Open Communication

Facilitating open communication involves encouraging honest expressions and confirming that everyone's voice is valued:

- Pose Open-Ended Questions: Encourage individuals to delve deeper into their thoughts by asking open-ended questions. For example, instead of asking, 'Did you enjoy the event?' one could prompt, 'What were your thoughts about the event?'

- Model Vulnerability: Leadership by example can be transformative. When leaders openly share their thoughts and feelings, it opens the door for others to do the same, establishing a deeper connection.
- Celebrate Contributions: Regular recognition of contributions, no matter how small, fosters motivation and encourages people to share more freely. For example, acknowledging someone's insight or thanking them for their honesty reinforces positive behaviour.

6. Handle Conflict with Care

Inevitably, conversations can spark disagreements. To maintain the integrity of safe spaces, learn to handle conflicts sensitively:

- Stay Calm: Respond to conflicts calmly. Your demeanour sets the tone; maintaining a composed attitude encourages others to feel less threatened.
- Practice Conflict Resolution: Utilize conflict-resolution strategies. Encourage collaborative problem-solving rather than punitive measures, which can undermine the safety of the space.

- Acknowledge Emotions: When conflicts arise, recognise the emotions involved. Validating feelings, even difficult ones, nurtures a sense of respect and safety.

7. *Continuously Check-In*

Communication is an ongoing process; checking in regularly reinforces the notion that everyone's input is valued:

- Establish Regular Feedback Sessions: Create opportunities for individuals to provide feedback on the conversational climate. Use anonymous surveys or direct discussions to gauge how safe participants feel.
- Adjust Accordingly: Be open to making adjustments based on feedback. Fostering a genuine willingness to improve reinforces trust and demonstrates commitment to creating a safe environment.
- Recognise growth: Celebrate progress in the dialogue processes. Acknowledging personal and group growth in communication abilities fosters motivation and continues the commitment to enhance the environment.

The Role of Faith in Creating Safe Spaces

For those who hold a faith perspective, integrating spiritual practices can further enrich the creation of safe spaces. Here are some ways faith can play a pivotal role:

- Prayer: Before engaging in deep conversations, invite participants to pray together. This fosters a shared intention of open-heartedness and support, providing divine guidance that can soften hearts and ears.
- Scriptural Reminders: Use scriptural passages that advocate for encouragement, understanding, and love as guiding principles during conversations. Verses like Ephesians 4:29—'Let no corrupting talk come out of your mouths, but only such as is good for building up, as fits the occasion, that it may give grace to those who hear'—serve as beautiful reminders of the power of uplifting speech.
- Emulating Christ's Example: Christ modelled unconditional love and understanding throughout His ministry. Encouraging participants to emulate His example can facilitate a culture that prioritises compassion and empathy.

Building Lasting Safe Spaces

Creating safe spaces is not a one-time effort but an ongoing commitment to fostering authentic dialogue.

- Develop a Culture: Strive to embed the principles of safety into the cultural fabric of your relationships. Eventually, conversations will naturally uphold the values you've cultivated, enabling ever-deepening connections.
- Encourage community: As individuals have positive experiences in safe spaces, encourage them to extend these values beyond initial settings. Sharing best practices across communities or groups helps expand the reach of safe dialogues and the nurturing relationships they foster.
- Remain Patient: Understand that building safe spaces takes time. When faced with setbacks, approach these challenges with patience and persistence, trusting that each effort contributes to collective healing.

In conclusion, the capacity to create safe spaces is a fundamental responsibility of each individual engaging in conversation. By investing in trust, empathy, and inclusivity, we foster environments that empower individuals to express their thoughts and feelings openly and honestly. This growth not only transforms conversations but also enhances the relationships we share. In a world often turbulent with discord, the power of creating safe spaces stands as a beacon of hope—a reminder that gentler breezes can often lead us toward greater harmony.

The Ripple Effect

In the quiet moments of reflection, we may recall experiences where a mere word or phrase sparked a cascade of emotions, thoughts, or even actions. Words have the striking ability to touch hearts, alter feelings, and even redirect lives. This is the ripple effect of our speech—a profound acknowledgement that every word we choose carries weight far beyond its immediate context. While a thought might only flicker like a candle's flame, words can ignite fireworks, creating ripples that extend into the lives of others in ways we might not fully comprehend.

Conversational impact begins with the realisation that our words are not isolated phenomena; they are embedded in a larger tapestry of human interaction. To fully appreciate their influence, we must cultivate Mindfulness in our speech. Mindfulness in conversation requires us to consider not just what we say, but how it may resonate with our listeners. It invites us to look beyond the surface of our dialogue and examine the deeper layers of communication that affect our connections.

The Power of Words

The metaphor of ripples in water serves as a poignant illustration of how words can extend into the lives of others. When a stone is thrown into a still pond, it creates a series of ripples that expand outward, touching the edges of the water and beyond. Similarly, our spoken words can initiate a chain reaction of thoughts and feelings in those who hear them. An encouraging word can light the way for someone struggling in darkness, while a careless comment can drench a moment of joy in sorrow. Understanding that our speech creates ripples empowers us to be more thoughtful and intentional in our communication.

To embrace this awareness, we first need to recognise how our words shape not only our relationships but also the environment around us. Consider the impact of kind words uttered in the right moment. 'You are valuable. Your contributions matter.' These affirmations, when expressed sincerely, resonate deeply within the listener's mind, bolstering confidence and inspiring positive action. Conversely, dismissive or cruel words can puncture a heart and create lasting scars. 'You are not good enough. You have failed again.' Such phrases can replay in an individual's psyche, acting as a stronghold of self-doubt.

In turbulent times, how often have individuals received an encouraging word that redirected their focus, ignited hope, or motivated them towards positive action? These instances illustrate that the ripples of our speech often reach further than we anticipate. The act of speaking uplifting words provides the recipient with a sense of belonging and validation. In doing so, we can help cultivate a culture where encouragement can flourish and where individuals feel empowered to shine.

Yet, it is not solely the uplifting words that affect our conversations. The power of our speech lies equally in our intentionality. When we speak with purpose and love, our words become a force for good, capable of fostering connection and understanding among diverse individuals. Each conversation presents an opportunity to deepen relationships, inspire collaboration, and foster a sense of community. However, it requires deliberate effort to engage thoughtfully in our dialogues. Choosing our words wisely, recognising the feelings of our audience, and being attuned to the emotional landscape of conversations is key in creating ripples that foster healing and not harm.

This intentional approach becomes particularly critical when we encounter challenging interactions. During conflicts or misunderstandings, the way we express ourselves can either escalate tension or pave the way for harmony. Words that are chosen mindfully, with empathy and a heart rooted in love, can create bridges even in the most turbulent waters of dialogue. Being deliberate does not mean stifling genuine expression; instead, it suggests a commitment to authenticity while allowing our conversations to be constructive and meaningful.

Examples abound of individuals whose mindful speech has changed the course of a conversation, leading to reconciliation rather than division. Consider a situation where two friends find themselves embroiled in a disagreement. Instead of resorting to defensive or accusatory language, one might pause and assertively state, 'I feel hurt because I felt left out of the decision-making process. Can we address how to include each other's perspectives next time?' This approach softens the conversation, reframing it from one of conflict to collaboration. The ripples from this intentional shift can be profound, engendering deeper trust and understanding.

An essential aspect of the ripple effect is the acknowledgement that people reflect what they receive. When individuals are met with kindness, they are often inspired to extend that kindness to others, perpetuating a cycle of positive interactions. A smile shared in passing may become the fuel that brightens another's day. An act of compassion can create a chain reaction that expands outwards, far beyond our immediate actions. This underscores the responsibility embedded in our ability to communicate. We must recognise the potential consequences of our words—not only for ourselves but for those within our sphere of influence.

Furthermore, the cascade of our words can have long-standing effects that echo into the future. An encouraging statement to a child can shape their self-perception for a lifetime, instilling resilience that drives them to pursue their dreams. Equally, negative comments can stifle aspirations and infuse self-doubt, influencing the trajectory of one's life. In this manner, the ripples of our words can last long after they are spoken, becoming woven into the fabric of someone's self-concept, aspirations, and overall outlook.

Given this understanding, it becomes vital to nurture a culture of encouragement. Encouragement transcends simple praise; it actively acknowledges the value of others and thus cultivates a supportive environment. When we engage in encouragement, we contribute to an atmosphere where individuals feel safe to experiment, to progress, and to support one another as they navigate life's challenges. While no one is immune to the trials of day-to-day existence, actively choosing our words can serve as a resilience-building exercise, fortifying our communities against despair and isolation.

However, lest we become naive, it is also essential to be aware of the darker side of conversational ripples. The potential for harm is equally present, where words can drown relationships instead of uplifting them. In moments of anger or frustration, careless words can create tumultuous waves that disrupt harmony, causing pain and confusion. Rumours spread like wildfire, distorting perceptions and creating barriers. The damage caused by harsh words can reverberate through communities, perpetuating conflict and division. In choosing our words, we must remember that the power to uplift exists alongside the power to tear down.

Consequently, cultivating a practice of reflection becomes invaluable. Assessing our words after a conversation enables us to evaluate their impact critically. Did our words uplift or cast shadows? Reflecting on these interactions can reveal patterns in our speech and illuminate areas for growth. Furthermore, creating an accountability structure with trusted friends or mentors can help foster this mindset; they can provide constructive feedback and offer insights into how our speech may resonate with others.

In the pursuit of impactful conversations, empathy serves as a guiding principle. Empathy enables us to recognise the potential effect of our words on another's heart and mind. When we listen and seek to understand before responding, we create an environment of mutual respect that fosters growth and development. Instead of approaching dialogue with a pre-structured response, we need to engage with our conversation partners genuinely. By dedicating time to listening, we invite compassion and understanding to inform our responses, leading to conversations that spread warmth rather than discord.

Additionally, it is beneficial to engage with intentional language scripts—specific phrases or affirmations we can draw upon to fortify our communication. Words of affirmation, compassion, and gratitude can be prepared ahead of time, equipping us with tools to enrich our conversations. When equipped with such language, we can transform even the most difficult dialogue into an opportunity for growth and understanding. Similarly, when it comes to speaking hard truths, being mindful of our tone and approach can help ensure that our intention—for healing and growth—shines through.

As we navigate daily interactions, we can also incorporate practices that enhance our consciousness of the ripple effect. Before entering a conversation, take a moment to centre yourself. This practice enables you to recognise your own emotions, allowing you to approach dialogue from a space of love rather than a reactive one. As you speak, commit to observing the nonverbal cues of your conversation partner and adjusting your approach based on their reactions. This flexibility in communication fosters authenticity and compassion, opening doors for deeper connections that extend well beyond the immediate moment.

The essence of living consciously through our words encourages us to communicate with intention in all forms of expression. Whether it is a simple greeting or a heartfelt confession, the ripples of our expressions have the potential to alter lives, weaving strands of connection across the tapestry of humanity. We can aspire to create waves of positivity and love by recognising our shared humanity and investing in our communication with intention.

Ultimately, the ripple effect is less about the magnitude of our words and more about their depth and resonance. It's the capacity for a few gentle words spoken genuinely in a moment of grace that can shift the trajectory of a conversation—and potentially a life. Instead of aiming for grand declarations, let us focus on fostering a legacy of kindness and connection. As we do, we can create ripples of love that spread through our communities, forging bonds of understanding, compassion, and encouragement.

In reflection, we must remember that every conversation is an opportunity for growth. With each word, we have the power to create ripples that shape our relationships and community. Embrace the responsibility of your speech, allowing love and Mindfulness to guide your words, and watch as these ripples connect the hearts of many. With conscious intent and compassionate dialogue, we can each contribute to a world that resonates with love, understanding, and grace.

Speak Life: The Essence of Encouragement

The Biblical Foundation of Encouragement

In our journey through life, we often encounter moments where a kind word, an uplifting thought, or an encouraging gesture can make all the difference. Scripture presents a rich tapestry of narratives that illustrate the profound impact of encouragement on individuals and communities alike. Among the many lessons woven throughout the biblical text, the theme of encouragement emerges as a powerful testament to the human experience, anchoring believers in their faith and fortifying them in their trials.

To understand the biblical foundation of encouragement, we must first explore the diverse array of characters who demonstrate its significance. These individuals, in their respective narratives, reveal the immense power of uplifting words and actions in faith-based interactions, helping us recognise how encouragement acts as a vehicle of divine grace that propels us toward growth, healing, and connection.

At the onset, let us turn our attention to the story of Moses, a figure marked by doubt and anxiety yet profoundly influenced by the encouragement of others. When tasked with leading the Israelites out of bondage in Egypt, Moses was not only hesitant but also overwhelmed by the weight of his divine calling. In Exodus 4, we witness Moses struggle with insecurity, voicing his concerns about his speaking ability and his worthiness to confront Pharaoh. It is here that God's encouragement manifests through the voice of Aaron, Moses' brother.

God, recognising Moses' anxious spirit, provided Aaron as a spokesperson, assuring Moses that he would not walk this path alone. This divine arrangement speaks volumes about the necessity of companionship in our journeys. God encouraged Moses by instilling confidence through the presence of a trusted ally. This powerful dynamic highlights a key principle within scripture: we are better together. Just as Aaron bolstered Moses' courage, we too can offer encouragement to our brothers and sisters, acting as instruments of God's grace and assurance.

For many of us, sharing our struggles can be a daunting task. The tale of David and Jonathan offers us another impactful exploration of encouragement in action. Their friendship, celebrated in 1 Samuel 18, stretches beyond mere kinship; it embodies loyalty, love, and mutual elevation. Following David's victory over Goliath, David's ascent to prominence threatened the established order, especially for Saul, Jonathan's father. Despite the potential conflict,

Jonathan's response was one of unwavering support and encouragement.

Jonathan recognised David's God-given potential and took steps to safeguard their bond, despite Saul's growing jealousy and animosity towards David. In 1 Samuel 23:16-17, Jonathan seeks David out in the wilderness, reminding him of the Lord's promises and reaffirming David's rightful place as king. His words were not mere platitudes; they were profound affirmations of faith that strengthened David's resolve during one of the most trying times of his life.

This narrative highlights that encouragement is not merely about offering praise, but instead signifies recognising the inherent worth and divine calling that each person carries. In our daily interactions, we must strive to emulate Jonathan's example by encouraging others through our words and actions, and by reflecting the understanding that each individual holds a unique path crafted by God.

The New Testament further expands on the significance of encouragement, calling believers to engage in this practice actively. In 1 Thessalonians 5:11, Paul urges the church to 'encourage one another and build each other up.' This command transcends mere verbal support; it embodies a lifestyle of encouragement that requires intentionality and effort. The church, as the body of Christ, is depicted as a community called to uplift its members, nurturing an environment of grace that allows individuals to flourish in their faith journeys.

The early church faced numerous challenges, from persecution to internal strife. In these turbulent times, encouragement became a vital lifeline, enabling believers to remain steadfast and united in the face of adversity. Paul himself exemplifies this principle through his letters, which often contained words of affirmation and hope. For instance, in Romans 12:10, he instructs believers to 'be devoted to one another in love. Honour one another above yourselves.' This passage serves as a call to action, urging us to prioritise the well-being of others, thus creating a nurturing cycle of encouragement that reflects the heart of Christ.

The parable of the Good Samaritan, found in Luke 10:25-37, provides another compelling example of encouragement through compassionate action. This story highlights the significance of deviating from societal norms to offer assistance and support. The Samaritan, moved by empathy and mercy, chose to support a beaten traveller when others passed him by. Here, we see that encouragement often requires practical action rather than just words. Our encouragement must translate into tangible acts of love, reaching out to those in need with open hearts and willing hands.

By examining these biblical narratives, we uncover a fundamental truth: encouragement fosters a sense of community. In a world increasingly marked by isolation and division, believers are called to cultivate environments in which encouragement flows freely. When we choose to speak life into the situations of others, we reflect the character of Christ, inviting His transformative presence into our interactions.

Furthermore, it is essential to recognise that the act of encouragement is not always natural. Our human tendencies may lead us to focus on criticism or comparison rather than affirmation. In this regard, the exhortation found in Ephesians 4:29 serves as a poignant reminder: 'Do not let any unwholesome talk come out of your mouths, but only what helps build others up according to their needs.' This scripture challenges us to guard our speech, ensuring that our words are infused with grace and aimed at fostering growth.

As we delve deeper into the biblical foundation of encouragement, we discover the profound role of personal testimony in uplifting others. Revelation 12:11 states, 'They triumphed over him by the blood of the Lamb and by the word of their testimony.' Sharing our stories of faith, struggle, and triumph can serve as a beacon of hope, lighting the way for those who may feel lost in their circumstances. When we recount our testimonies, we create a powerful link between our experiences and God's faithfulness, building bridges of understanding and empathy.

Consider the testimony of Peter, who, despite his faltering moments, emerged as a resilient leader in the early church. After denying Christ, Peter was restored in a profoundly personal encounter with Jesus (John 21:15-17). This restoration allowed him to encourage others who faced moments of doubt and failure. His journey reminds us that encouragement is often rooted in our vulnerabilities and the willingness to embrace our brokenness.

The ancient wisdom found in Proverbs also contributes to our understanding of the power of encouragement. Proverbs 16:24 states, 'Gracious words are a honeycomb, sweet to the soul and healing to the bones.' When we choose our words wisely, we cultivate an atmosphere of encouragement that nourishes those around us, much like honey brings sweetness and healing. It is an invitation to reflect on the types of words we speak and their potential impact on our relationships.

Ultimately, encouragement is a divine calling that urges us to reflect God's heart towards others. As we explore the vast landscape of scripture, we see that encouragement moves beyond mere sentiment; it is an active pursuit of building others up and instilling hope. Understanding that our words hold power emphasises the biblical mandate to be vessels of encouragement woven intricately into the fabric of our faith.

As we conclude this exploration of the biblical foundation of encouragement, let us commit to embracing the call to uplift one another. May we take inspiration from the myriad examples found in scripture and acknowledge our role in fostering an environment where encouragement thrives. Words can heal, empower, and transform, echoing the love of Christ that dwells within us. Let us choose to speak life into every interaction, embodying the essence of encouragement in our daily lives, and allowing the Holy Spirit to guide our speech and actions. In doing so, we honour God's design for community and reflect the beautiful tapestry of His love.

To embody encouragement authentically, let us remember the words of Colossians 3:12-14, which remind us to clothe ourselves in compassion, kindness, humility, gentleness, and patience. When we approach one another with these virtues, we cultivate relationships that mirror the heart of God. Encouragement, rooted in these characteristics, becomes a powerful tool for building unity in faith and nurturing the bonds that hold us together as a body.

In the grand narrative of the Bible, encouragement is intricately woven through the lives of characters who exemplify the profound impact of uplifting words. Our call to fill the world with encouragement is not merely a suggestion; it is a command steeped in the fabric of our faith. As we step into this vital role, let us be mindful of our words and eager to empower one another, partnering with God in His healing work.

As a community, let us engage in practices that uplift and inspire one another. Whether through speaking affirmations, offering a listening ear, or providing overt support during trying times, we embody the essence of encouragement that mirrors the heart of our Creator. By doing so, we are poised to transform our relationships, our communities, and ultimately, our world, reminding one another of the divine potential that resides within us all. Let's be relentless in our pursuit of encouragement, cultivating a culture of kindness and support that resonates within the hearts of those around us, as we champion the message: Speak life, and watch it flourish.

Crafting Words of Life

In the journey of cultivating a culture of encouragement, it becomes essential to understand the power of language and its ability to create an atmosphere of life and vitality. In this subchapter, we will delve deep into the art of crafting words that not only uplift but also inspire those around us. Crafting Words of Life becomes a vital skill that allows us to harness the transformative potential of our speech, turning simple phrases into beacons of hope, love, and affirmation.

To effectively engage in this process, we can begin by identifying the core characteristics of encouraging speech—authenticity, clarity, and intent. As we navigate through practical exercises and specific phrases, we will build an arsenal of words that resonate deeply with the essence of encouragement.

Understanding the Impact of Words

Before we dive into crafting articulations of life, let's consider the impact of words on our relationships and the atmosphere around us. Proverbs 18:21 tells us that 'the tongue has the power of life and death, and those who love it will eat its fruit.' This biblical wisdom highlights the critical role our speech plays in shaping environments and relationships. When we choose our words wisely, we foster a culture of encouragement and support; careless speech, on the other hand, can lead to hurt and disengagement.

Furthermore, our words should reflect our intentions. An insightful understanding of this principle can motivate us to craft expressions that hold the potential to uplift. To ignite this process, we will engage in a series of exercises designed to enhance our vocabulary while instilling the essence of life into our conversations.

The Power of Words

Exercise 1: The Encouragement Journals

The first exercise involves maintaining an Encouragement Journal. This journal will act as a repository for inspiration, allowing you to jot down specific phrases, affirmations, and thoughts that emerge during your daily interactions or that resonate with you in any moment of inspiration.

1. Allocate Time Daily: Set aside a few moments each day to write in your journal. Reflect on your day's interactions or moments where you encountered uplifting phrases.

2. Capture Affirmations: Write down phrases that stand out to you as particularly encouraging. These can be quotes from scriptures, inspiring messages from books, profound statements from friends, or even your thoughts and reflections.

3. Compile Personal Models: Consider adding to your journal phrases that you believe could encourage others in specific situations—for example, uplifting phrases for friends facing challenges or encouragement for colleagues at work.

4. Create Themes: To better harness the power of these expressions later, categorise them by themes such as gratitude, resilience, challenges, and hope. This will make it easier to draw from them when the need arises.

Exercise 2: Word Crafting Workshops

Next, we introduce the Word Crafting Workshop—an exercise designed for personal reflection and group dynamics. This collaborative approach will enhance your ability to practice encouraging speech with a community.

1. Gather a Group: Consider inviting a few friends or family members who value encouragement to join you in this workshop.

2. Setting the Ground Rules: Create an atmosphere of trust and openness, establishing that the purpose of the workshop is to uplift and support one another.

3. Choose a Theme: Each session, select a theme such as 'Overcoming Fear' or 'Building Hope.' This theme will guide the crafting of your words.

4. Practice Phrasing: Take turns sharing personal experiences related to the theme. As individuals share, the group will collaboratively generate encouraging phrases and affirmations that align with each story.

5. Document the Craft: Write down the crafted phrases and revisit them during future workshops to celebrate the growth in your collective ability to encourage.

Specific Phrases to Inspire

Now that we have established a foundation with these exercises, let's explore some specific phrases and affirmations that embody encouragement, empowering your communicative efforts. Having a collection of these phrases can significantly enhance your ability to bring life to your interactions.

1. Affirmations for Self-Love:

- 'You are created beautifully and wonderfully; embrace who you are.'
- 'Your value is not based on achievements; it exists simply because you are you.'

2. Encouragement During Difficult Times:

- 'Every storm eventually passes; you are resilient and will find calm once again.'
- 'You are not alone in this; I am here for you every step of the way.'

3. Motivational Messages for Growth:

- 'Mistakes are simply stepping stones on the path to greatness; keep moving forward.'

- 'Growth occurs outside of comfort; lean into the challenges before you.'

4. Expressions of Gratitude:

- 'I appreciate your one-of-a-kind perspective; it enriches our conversations.'
- 'Thank you for your kindness; your actions ripple positively through those around you.'

These phrases serve as a simple yet powerful foundation for building meaningful exchanges that foster encouragement and uplift others.

Exercise 3: The 30-Day Encouragement Challenge

To further reinforce this practice, engage in the 30-Day Encouragement Challenge. Each day, you will focus on crafting and sharing an encouraging message with a different person.

1. Day 1: Reflect on your day and draft a message centred on gratitude directed to a colleague for their efforts.

2. Day 2: Focus on your family members. Write a personal note affirming each family member's strengths.

3. Continue the Journey: Each day, select a different recipient—friends, community members, or even social media connections—and share your encouragement.

4. Document Responses: Keep track of their responses, noticing the ways your words impacted them. This awareness encourages us to be more intentional in our speech moving forward.

Building an Arsenal of Words

As you embark on this journey, continually add to your artillery of encouraging phrases. Each phrase you craft should resonate with authenticity and stem from genuine emotion. The more you practice, the more your ability to uplift through speech will develop. Follow these strategies to expand your collection:

1. Read and Reflect: Explore literature, poetry, and scriptures that inspire your inner voice toward encouragement. Write down phrases that speak to you.

2. Practice Daily Affirmations: Begin each day with affirmations dedicated to yourself. The habit of affirming your worth and abilities will enable you to pass on that kindness to others.

3. Engage with Feedback: Don't hesitate to ask those whom you encourage how your words resonated with them. This feedback

could inform your future crafting efforts and enhance the specificity of your expressions.

The Power of Context in Communication

It's crucial to remember that the impact of words lies not only in the phrases themselves but also in their context. The emotion behind your delivery, the timing of your encouragement, and your body language all contribute to how effectively your message is received. Here are some pointers to ensure your words land well:

1. Know Your Audience: Tailor your messages to the specific needs of the person you are encouraging. Be aware of what challenges they might face and how your words could meet them in that space.

2. Use Active Listening: Engage sincerely in conversations with others. This not only informs you on how to encourage them better but also reassures them that they are heard and understood.

3. Be Present: Discounts or distractions lead to disconnection. When you express encouragement, make it a priority to be fully present with the other person, enhancing the emotional impact of your words.

Harnessing the Divine in Our Daily Speech

As believers, we can recognise that our ability to craft life-giving words is inherently connected to our faith. In James 1:17, we read that every good and perfect gift is from above, implying that the gift of encouraging speech is a manifestation of divine love and grace. As we cultivate this talent, we not only serve those around us but also honour the divine source of our expressions.

Let us remember that crafting words of life transcends mere encouragement; it reflects the character of Christ in us. Each kind word we speak carries the weight of His love and compassion. Therefore, strive not just to speak encouraging words, but to engage in a deep connection through the lens of faith that binds us together.

Conclusion: Embracing the Journey of Crafting Words

In closing, the commitment to crafting words of life is both a personal and communal journey. By integrating practical exercises into our daily lives and building an arsenal of uplifting phrases, we reshape our environments to speak life into them.

Embrace the enlightening experiences that come from practising encouragement as a vital part of your communication.

Reflect on the goodness of speech as a divine instrument designed to uplift, inspire, and build others into their fullness of potential. With every word spoken, aspire to spread joy, hope, and the warmth of encouragement, truly harnessing the power of your words to have a generational impact.

Embracing Vulnerability

In a world often marked by strength and bravado, vulnerability can feel like a daunting endeavour. However, it is precisely this openness—this willingness to show our authentic selves—that has the power to foster genuine connections and cultivate an environment of encouragement. Embracing vulnerability in our interactions not only reshapes our relationships but also allows encouragement to flourish in ways we may not have previously imagined.

At its core, vulnerability is about authenticity. It calls us to let down our defences, to reveal our true selves—flaws, fears, dreams, and all. It is the breath of courage that whispers, 'I am enough, just as I am.' In moments of vulnerability, we create a space where others feel safe to share their own stories. This mutual exchange becomes a catalyst for encouragement, as authenticity begets authenticity.

Studies have shown that when individuals express their vulnerabilities, it can significantly change the dynamics of their relationships. People are naturally drawn to those who display a genuine sense of self. This occurs because vulnerability fosters connection; it resonates with our shared human experience. When we share our struggles, triumphs, and the sometimes messy reality of life, we create a bond that is anchored in trust and relatability.

Consider a moment from the life of a beloved mentor or friend. When they opened up about their struggles, did it not deepen your admiration and respect for them? You likely felt a sense of kinship, realising you were not alone in facing your challenges. This is the essence of vulnerability—it invites others into our lives and emphasises that we are all in this journey together.

To embrace vulnerability, one must first recognise what it means to be vulnerable. It is not about airing our deepest secrets or laying bare every shameful thought; rather, it is about sharing our experiences in a manner that reveals our humanity. This can be as simple as expressing how we feel after a tough day or confessing our fears about the future. It allows for a connection that transcends the superficiality so often found in daily interactions.

As we navigate relationships—whether with friends, family, co-workers, or strangers—taking the step toward vulnerability can seem intimidating. The fear of being judged is a significant barrier that many face. We may worry that if we share our true selves, we will be met with criticism or rejection. However, embracing vulnerability can create an environment where criticism is reduced. When we lead with our hearts open, others tend to respond with empathy and understanding rather than judgment.

Moreover, the act of sharing heart-centred vulnerabilities can serve as an encouragement itself. When we are open about our struggles, others may find the courage to reveal their own. Consider the profound impact that a simple admission can have: 'I am struggling with fear,' or 'I feel overwhelmed.' Such statements open the door for compassion and support, creating a cascading effect of encouragement.

Reflection also plays a crucial role in vulnerability. When we ponder our own experiences, we begin to understand our emotions more clearly. This understanding can then be translated into our interactions with others, enriching our conversations with depth and authenticity. Each interaction becomes an opportunity to practice vulnerability and, in doing so, form a tapestry of shared experiences that spans across various contexts.

As we delve into the biblical perspective of vulnerability, we see that even esteemed figures in scripture were not shy about expressing their struggles. David, the king of Israel, penned the Psalms with raw emotion, detailing his fears, doubts, and heartfelt pleas to God. He invites readers into a deeply vulnerable space where lament meets hope, demonstrating that vulnerability is an integral component of faith.

Philippians 4:6-7 encourages us with the words of the apostle Paul when he instructs us not to be anxious but to present our requests to God with thanksgiving. This act of presenting our vulnerabilities and concerns is an embodiment of trust, both in God and in ourselves. When we acknowledge our need for support, we enter into a reciprocal relationship where encouragement can flourish.

The power of vulnerability extends beyond our personal experiences; it also plays a significant role in nurturing communities. Vulnerability can serve as a foundation for group dynamics, be it in a church, a family, or any community. Encouragement flourishes when individuals share their authentic selves; it builds a safe space where others feel empowered to do the same. This shared vulnerability reinforces a sense of belonging, of being seen and heard.

In the context of encouragement, consider how often a simple acknowledgement of struggle can uplift others. For instance, in group settings, sharing personal challenges or experiences can catalyse a collective sense of support. When one person speaks from a place of vulnerability, it often prompts others to remove their masks of perfection and reveal their authentic selves. This cycle of sharing can lead to profound healing and encouragement.

Moreover, we can integrate practical approaches to embrace vulnerability within our lives. Start by creating a safe environment for open dialogue. Whether this takes the shape of family dinners where feelings are shared or casual meetups with friends where honest conversations flow, it is essential to find spaces that nurture vulnerability. In these environments, encourage dialogues that explore feelings rather than simply exchanging surface-level pleasantries. This shift helps to answer the unspoken question: 'Is it safe for me to be vulnerable here?'

Practising mindfulness can also enhance our ability to embrace vulnerability. Being mindful means being present, aware, and in tune with our thoughts and feelings. This practice equips us to recognise moments where vulnerability could enhance connections. By taking a deep breath and checking in with our emotional state, we can choose to speak from a place of authenticity, even when fear lurks in the corners of our hearts.

Furthermore, the words we choose play a crucial role in cultivating an atmosphere of encouragement through vulnerability. Speaking kindly, affirming others' worth, and expressing gratitude can serve as gentle nudges that promote a culture of openness and trust. When we use language that reflects acceptance and warmth, it encourages others to share their vulnerabilities without fear of rejection.

The transformation of relationships through this cycle of vulnerability and encouragement can be profound. By embracing the imperfections of being human, we allow ourselves to connect with others on a deeper level. We confront the barriers of loneliness, isolation, and doubt, replacing them with community, support, and love.

In conclusion, embracing vulnerability in our interactions is a transformative practice that is essential for fostering genuine encouragement. In a world that often prioritises strength and the facade of perfection, vulnerability opens doors to authentic connections and vital conversations. We stand to empower not only ourselves but also those around us when we accept the risk of vulnerability. As we communicate from our authentic selves, we challenge others to do the same, creating an encouraging tapestry woven through love, honesty, and mutual support. Let us choose

The Power of Words

vulnerability as a pathway to encouragement, enabling our words to resonate deeply and create lasting impacts in our relationships.

Harbours of Harmony: Navigating Conflict Through Communication

Anchoring Empathy

In a world rife with conflicts both big and small, the power of empathy emerges as a beacon of hope—a steadfast anchor in turbulent waters. It holds the potential to transform heated discussions into constructive conversations and de-escalate tensions, fostering an environment where understanding prevails over resentment. This subchapter seeks to elucidate the pivotal role empathy plays in navigating the stormy seas of conflict, guiding individuals toward productive dialogue and deeper connections.

To truly grasp the significance of empathy in communication, we must first establish what empathy is. At its core, empathy is the ability to perceive and feel another person's emotions, allowing one to stand alongside the other rather than in opposition. It requires vulnerability, a willingness to listen, and an open heart that draws upon grace and understanding. In contrast to sympathy, which often keeps a distance by pitying another's situation, empathy allows for a shared experience—a profound connection that can disarm hostility and promote healing.

The Power of Words

Picture a scenario in which two friends, Sarah and Emily, find themselves in a heated argument. Sarah feels unheard and belittled in their discussions, while Emily believes she is merely sharing her opinion. Each person's perspective seems valid, and yet their emotions drive them increasingly apart. As voices rise and tempers flare, this conflict embodies the typical pattern seen in many relationships: misunderstandings escalate into full-blown arguments, often causing irreparable damage.

But here's where empathy can change the narrative. What if, instead of raising their voices, Sarah and Emily paused and actively sought to understand each other's feelings? If Sarah had the courage to express, 'I feel unvalued when you dismiss my thoughts, and it makes me frustrated,' while Emily clarified, 'I didn't intend to belittle your opinions. I just wanted to share mine because I care about our discussion.' This exchange, wrapped in empathy, fosters an environment where healing occurs, and their relationship can grow stronger rather than fracture further.

Empathy anchors our conversations by establishing a common ground. When we approach conflict with the intent to understand, we create a safe space for vulnerability. Individuals are more likely to share their feelings, thoughts, and concerns honestly when they sense that their counterpart is genuinely listening to them. The two-way street of communication acts like a bridge spanning an emotional chasm, drawing participants closer together.

In this light, it's important to note that empathy is not a natural inclination for everyone, primarily in high-stress situations. Our instincts might nudge us toward defensiveness or aggression when someone challenges our views. Therefore, to cultivate empathy as an anchor, we must first practice self-awareness, acknowledging our emotional triggers and responses during conflicts. This self-awareness enables us to pause, breathe, and intentionally choose empathy over reaction.

Taking a moment to breathe deeply and gather our thoughts allows empathy to emerge. Engaging in mindfulness practices can further enhance our capacity for empathy. Delving deep into our thoughts, feeling the sensations of our bodies, we can recognise where our emotions stem from. When we learn to observe our feelings without acting upon them, we create an opportunity to separate our own experience from that of the other person.

Consider the role of patience in this equation, as it complements empathy beautifully. Patience gives us the time to listen, reflect, and understand before responding. When embroiled in conflict, our instinct may lead us to respond quickly, hoping to justify our position or defend ourselves. However, taking a pause can allow the tides of emotion to settle, helping us listen more effectively and respond in ways that are thoughtful and constructive, rather than impulsive and reactive.

Now, let's explore how, through empathetic dialogue, we can foster connection even amid conflict. When engaging with another, we can utilise active listening—focusing on the other person's words and emotional state without formulating our response until they have finished expressing themselves. This practice not only communicates our desire to understand but also creates a space where the other person feels heard and validated. It's important to use affirming body language, maintain eye contact, and avoid distractions. Every nod and reassuring glance reinforce their willingness to connect.

Inherent within each conversation are different layers of meaning. Words encapsulate emotions, histories, and perspectives forged in personal experiences—elements we often overlook in the heat of argument. When we listen empathetically, we peel away the layers, revealing the deeper emotions beneath the surface. For instance, a seemingly aggressive tone may mask underlying fear or insecurity. Through empathetic listening, we can help each other explore those hidden emotions, transforming misunderstanding into insight.

Moreover, empathy invites vulnerability—an essential component for resolution. When one party leads with vulnerability, it encourages the other to do the same. Sarah may express her feelings of pain and exclusion without fear of judgment, opening the door for Emily's authentic self-exploration. Vulnerability breaks down defensive barriers, allowing for raw expressions of humanity that ultimately strengthen relationships.

However, the journey toward empathetic conflict resolution isn't without challenges. Let's acknowledge that sometimes, we may encounter individuals who are not ready or willing to engage empathetically, either due to their own emotional turmoil or lack of awareness. Nurturing empathy within ourselves does not guarantee the same from others; yet, we can still model the behaviour we wish to see.

The story of a mediator might resonate here. Picture a skilled mediator stepping into a workplace conflict. While one party expresses frustration regarding a lack of communication, the other may resent feeling blamed. In such a scenario, the mediator, trained in empathy-led techniques, reflects on the feelings of each party. By voicing both sides' emotions without bias, the mediator can reframe the discussion—leading to a collective problem-solving approach rather than a blame game.

The Power of Words

The significant takeaway here is that while empathy can anchor our conversations, it also requires practice—a muscle we strengthen over time. Building empathy often starts with a conscious choice that we make daily, in routine conversations and interactions. When we choose to listen deeply, reflect, and respond intentionally, we begin to cultivate a culture of empathy not only within ourselves but also in our relationships as a whole.

Encouraging empathy integrates seamlessly into daily interactions. When we encounter differing opinions or unmet needs in a relationship, we can ask ourselves: 'What might they be feeling right now?' This inquiry opens pathways to understanding, guiding us toward reactions rooted in compassion.

Let's discuss one more essential aspect—naming emotions. When we identify and articulate emotions during conflicts, we provide both ourselves and the other party with context. Phrases such as 'I sense that you're feeling hurt or frustrated' help validate feelings rather than dismiss them. It encourages the emotional exchange that builds bridges amid clashes. Taking a moment to say, 'I see you're upset. Let's talk about what's bothering you,' can go a long way in softening tense situations and promoting dialogue focused on resolution.

The Power of Words

Grounding ourselves in empathy also enhances our emotional intelligence. It strengthens relationships by fostering deeper connections based on authenticity, trust, and mutual respect. The benefits extend beyond our immediate relationships to encompass our families, workplaces, and the broader community. As we anchor our communication in empathy, we are, in essence, creating a ripple effect—encouraging others to adopt the same practices, leading to healthier and more harmonious interactions.

Finally, let's consider the broader implications of empathetic conflict resolution. As we bring empathy into our interactions, we contribute to a culture that values understanding over division and reconciliation over hostility. We can collectively elevate our conversations by focusing on compassion, thereby lifting communities.

In summary, empathy is an anchor—an essential element that fosters understanding, patience, and productive dialogue in the face of conflict. The possibility of transforming our disputes into opportunities for growth lies within our ability to cultivate empathy. Through intentional practices of active listening, vulnerability, naming emotions, and self-awareness, we anchor ourselves in compassion and create environments where relationships can flourish instead of fracture.

Through each interaction infused with empathy, we collectively weave a legacy of love—a testament to the grace we extend toward one another in our human experiences. Thus, let us embark on this journey, championing empathy as our anchor, inviting our relationships into the harbours of harmony.

The Art of Deliberate Speech

In the man-made cacophony of our everyday lives, many of us experience conflict as a familiar yet distressing occurrence. The subtle tensions simmer beneath the surface of relationships, often escalating into misunderstandings that could have been easily avoided. In these heated moments, it is crucial to remember the importance of deliberate speech. Our words are powerful agents of change; they carry the potential to either escalate a situation or bring about healing and resolution. Thus, understanding the art of choosing our words carefully can pave the way to harmony, not just in conflicts, but in all our interactions.

Deliberate speech requires intentionality—using words that reflect thoughtfulness, compassion, and clarity. It invites us to step back from our emotions, to pause before reacting impulsively, and to be mindful of the impact of our words. In learning to harness this skill, we cultivate not only a sense of responsibility for our own communication but also a greater empathy toward those with whom we interact. This journey into deliberate speech will explore various techniques that can help us navigate conflict gracefully.

The Foundation of Deliberate Speech

To embark on this journey, we must first understand what we mean by 'deliberate speech.' At its core, this concept revolves around the conscious choice of language that aligns with our values and intentions. Deliberate speech reflects an awareness of the context of our conversations, recognising that our words can transform a disagreement into an opportunity for deeper understanding.

Consider the metaphor of a ship navigating through treacherous waters. A skilled captain does not leave the course to chance; instead, she relies on her compass, understands the winds and tides, and adjusts her sails to reach her destination safely. Similarly, deliberate speech requires an understanding of our internal compass—our values, principles, and the ultimate goals we seek in our communications.

In moments of conflict, it is essential to anchor ourselves in these values. We must ask ourselves: What do I wish to achieve through this conversation? Am I seeking understanding, reconciliation, or simply the validation of my perspective? When we approach communication with clarity about our intentions, our words take on a purposeful quality that can defuse tension and foster dialogue.

Recognising Emotional Triggers

Conflict often elicits strong emotions—such as anger, frustration, and disappointment—which can cloud our judgment and lead to unintentional harm. A crucial first step in mastering deliberate speech is recognising our emotional triggers. Emotions serve as signals, informing us about our responses to specific situations or behaviours. Understanding what triggers our emotions allows us to pause and recalibrate before responding.

For example, let's say a colleague interrupts you during a meeting, triggering feelings of frustration and resentment due to a longstanding pattern of behaviour. If left unaddressed, this frustration may manifest in a defensive or accusatory tone, which will likely escalate the conflict. Instead, by acknowledging that the interruption triggers strong feelings in you, you can take a deep breath and choose to respond more thoughtfully.

Earlier, we drew a parallel between conflict and navigating seas. Just as a sailor may learn to read the signs of impending storms, we too can become adept at recognising the signs of our emotional storms. We can train ourselves to take a moment, engage in self-reflection, and consider our desired outcome. This may mean formulating a response that expresses how the interruption made you feel while also inviting collaboration rather than confrontation.

Practising Active Listening

Active listening is an essential companion of deliberate speech. It is a practice rooted in empathy, requiring us to fully engage with the speaker's message rather than merely preparing our counters or responses. By employing active listening, we validate the speaker's experience, fostering a more respectful dialogue.

When engaged in a conflict, offer your full attention to the other person. Maintain eye contact, nod occasionally, and refrain from interrupting. Use reflective techniques, such as paraphrasing what they have said, to ensure understanding. For instance, you can say, 'What I hear you saying is that you felt ignored when I interrupted you. Is that correct?' This approach not only helps clarify the speaker's concerns but also shows respect for their feelings.

Moreover, behind every conflict often lies a more profound need or desire—be it validation, respect, or understanding. By actively listening, you begin to unearth these underlying needs, allowing you to address the root of the conflict rather than merely its symptoms. Deliberate communication, therefore, is as much about what we say as about how we choose to listen.

Choosing Words Wisely

Every word we choose carries weight, and it can lead to differing interpretations based on context and tone. Therefore, using precise and clear language is crucial, particularly in emotionally charged situations. Avoid ambiguous language that may be misconstrued. Instead of saying, 'You always dismiss my ideas,' you might say, 'I feel my contributions have not been acknowledged in our discussions.' This approach does not place blame directly on the other person but instead shares your feelings and invites dialogue.

Additionally, using 'I' statements rather than 'you' statements can minimise defensiveness. For example, framing your feelings with an 'I' statement—'I feel hesitant to share my ideas when they are interrupted'—focuses on personal feelings rather than accusatory language that can alienate the other person. This technique encourages empathy and fosters a sense of shared understanding, distancing both parties from feelings of attack.

The Pause Principle

Implementing a 'pause principle' during conflict can significantly enhance the effectiveness of your communication. Often, conflict triggers a quick-fire exchange of words that can lead to escalating tension rather than resolution. By consciously choosing to pause—taking a deep breath or stepping back for a moment—you can avoid reacting in anger and instead respond thoughtfully.

This pause allows you to evaluate your feelings, articulate your needs, and gather clarity on how to express them. Consider this an opportunity to formulate a response that aligns with your core values and intentions. Instead of retaliating, you may choose to share your struggles, ensuring both parties get a chance to express their side without escalating the discord.

Empathising with the Other Party

Walking a mile in someone else's shoes requires an active choice to understand their perspective, especially in the face of conflict. Empathy enables us to understand the intricacies of another person's experiences, emotions, and motivations. This process not only helps reduce our own emotional reactions but also fosters a more collaborative approach.

When you empathise, the other person may have also responded out of their fears, misunderstandings, or insecurities. Engaging in dialogue that acknowledges their struggles can pave the way for vulnerability on both sides. Educate yourself in the art of empathy by asking clarifying questions, such as, 'Can you share what led you to feel that way?' This inquiry demonstrates genuine interest and can foster a connection that replaces defensiveness with mutual respect.

The Role of Nonverbal Communication

Our words are amplified or diminished by our nonverbal cues. Body language, facial expressions, and tone of voice play a significant role in shaping the perception of our message. Therefore, it is vital to align your verbal and nonverbal communication in a way that enhances clarity rather than muddling it.

In an argument, maintaining a calm tone and open posture can help de-escalate potential tension. Conversely, crossing your arms or using a harsh tone can signal defensiveness or hostility, prompting the other person to react similarly. Here, we emphasise the need for awareness of our body language—maintaining eye contact, using gestures that invite openness, and keeping an even tone—as these factors are as significant as the words we choose to deliver.

Reframing Conflict as Opportunity

Informed by the practices of deliberate speech, it can be transformative to view conflict not as a harbinger of doom but as an opportunity for growth and learning. Every disagreement holds within it a chance for greater understanding, a pathway for strengthening relationships, and a platform for shared insights.

To draw from our earlier metaphor of navigating through waters, conflict can be likened to the occasionally fierce tempest. In the midst of these storms, we are given the chance to hone our navigational skills. Each conflict contributes to our ability to manoeuvre future conversations with greater grace. By reframing conflict, we shift our mindset from defining it as a confrontation to an opportunity for resolution, connection, and growth.

Creating a Culture of Deliberate Speech

As individuals, we contribute to the larger dynamics of our relational spheres. Thus, extending the practice of deliberate speech beyond ourselves can cultivate a culture of open dialogue and respect in families, workplaces, and communities. This involves modelling the techniques we have explored—choosing words mindfully, practising active listening, and fostering empathy—while also encouraging others to do the same.

Lead by example; share your experiences of navigating conflict through deliberate speech. When we acknowledge the positive outcomes of thoughtful communication, we inspire others to follow suit. Encourage workshops or discussions that centre on communication skills within your community or organisation, creating shared platforms for dialogue that can break down barriers.

Conclusion: A Lifelong Commitment

Perfecting the art of deliberate speech is not an overnight achievement; it is a lifelong commitment that requires practice, patience, and persistence. We remind ourselves that each conflict presents an opportunity to refine our approach, drawing forth the lessons from our conversations.

In the tapestry of relationships that we weave, deliberate speech acts as the thread uniting disparate colours and patterns. By embodying clear, compassionate communication during conflicts, we weave a fabric of understanding that can beautifully transform our world, ushering us toward harmony rather than discord.

Ultimately, the commitment to deliberate speech empowers us to navigate life's turbulent seas with greater ease and grace. As we encourage and uplift one another through our words, we fulfil our higher calling to represent love and truth, creating spaces where trust and understanding can flourish.

Building Bridges, Not Walls

In our interconnected world, conflict is a natural occurrence—an inevitable part of our relationships and interactions. It can arise from misunderstandings, differing values, or opposing opinions. However, instead of recoiling from conflict or viewing it as a negative experience, we have the opportunity to see it as a catalyst for growth and reconciliation. In this subchapter, we will explore actionable steps to resolve conflicts, with a focus on rebuilding trust and fostering connection.

The first step in navigating conflict is to embrace it with an open heart and a humble spirit. Recognising that conflict can lead to understanding and growth requires a shift in perspective. When we change how we view conflict, we begin to see that each disagreement offers a chance to deepen our connections with others while examining our motivations and the beliefs we hold. When approached with this mindset, conflict becomes a mechanism for healthy communication rather than an adversarial struggle.

One effective technique to initiate this process is to engage in active listening. This is not merely hearing the words spoken but fully absorbing the emotion and intention behind them. Active listening requires concentration and effort; it calls for us to set aside our preconceived notions and actively focus on understanding the other party's viewpoint.

To practice active listening:

1. Maintain Eye Contact: This conveys attentiveness and respect.

2. Avoid Interrupting: Let the other person finish their thoughts before responding.

3. Reflect: Paraphrase what you have heard to ensure clarity and understanding. For example, you might say, 'What I hear you saying is…' This shows that you are engaged in the dialogue and genuinely care to comprehend their perspective.

4. Ask Open-Ended Questions: Instead of leading questions that might steer the conversation toward a specific outcome, encourage deeper exploration. For instance, ask, 'How did that situation make you feel?' This will provoke thoughtful responses and deeper insights into the speaker's state of mind.

After implementing active listening, creating a safe space for dialogue is crucial. A 'safe space' allows individuals to express their thoughts and feelings without fear of judgment or retribution. Techniques for fostering this environment include:

- **Setting Ground Rules:** Agree on a set of guidelines for discussions, such as no name-calling, allowing time for each person to speak, and refraining from dismissive body language.
- **Encouraging Empathy:** Remind participants to express empathy towards one another. Phrases such as 'I can understand why you might feel that way' can bridge gaps in understanding.
- **Using Timed Responses:** Allocate a specific amount of time for each participant to express their views, ensuring that everyone feels heard and valued.

Once a safe environment has been established, the next step in resolving conflict is to identify the root cause of the disagreement. Often, conflicts can be a symptom of underlying issues rather than the issue itself. Encouraging open and honest conversation can bring these underlying feelings to the forefront. Ask questions aimed at seeking deeper insights, such as:

- What specific actions or words triggered this conflict?

- How can we work together to find a resolution?

- Is there a pattern to our disagreements?

Recognising patterns in conflicts can help individuals understand their triggers and responses better. By addressing recurring issues, we may begin to dismantle the walls that conflict has built over time. Rather than simply putting a Band-Aid on the immediate disagreement, we can tackle the underlying causes contributing to the conflict.

Once we have identified the reasons for conflict, we can work together to find solutions. Collaboration rather than confrontation fosters a spirit of reconciliation and teamwork. Here are some strategies to facilitate collaborative problem-solving:

- **Brainstorm Solutions Together:** Rather than proposing solutions unilaterally, engage all parties in brainstorming ideas that might satisfy everyone involved. This can create a sense of ownership and investment in the solution.
- **Negotiate: Be open to compromise.** Acknowledge that not everyone might get exactly what they want, but that the common goal is to resolve the disagreement.
- **Focus on Interests Not Positions:** Instead of debating specific positions, explore the interests behind those positions. This reframing can lead to

creative solutions that satisfy underlying needs rather than taking a rigid stance.

Communication is crucial, but resolving conflicts also requires accountability and commitment to change. After reaching an agreement or solution, individual commitments should be documented. This could be archived in the form of notes or a signed contract that articulates the pathways forward. This step provides clarity and reinforces trust, demonstrating that all parties are committed to fulfilling the commitments they have made.

Trust-building exercises can further enhance relationships after a conflict. These exercises may include a variety of strategies designed to foster goodwill:

- **Affirming Words:** Commit to speaking positively about each other when discussing the conflict with others.
- **Quality Time:** Spend time together engaging in enjoyable activities that enhance connection and reinforce your commitment to each other's well-being.
- **Regular Check-ins:** Set aside time regularly to discuss how each party is feeling about the relationship and any emerging concerns.

Additionally, it is essential to recognise that resolving conflict is not a one-time event, but a continuous process. Building rapport and goodwill can take time, so patience is vital. Acknowledging this and committing to the journey ahead is essential for rebuilding connections.

Honouring the journey doesn't negate the reality of feelings or experiences. Conflict can elicit strong emotions such as anger, frustration, and disappointment. It is important for those involved to express these feelings honestly to one another—and with respect. Resisting the impulse to suppress emotions allows the healing process to begin, creating space for forgiveness to enter the dialogue.

In instances where conflict feels insurmountable, seeking mediation can also prove beneficial. An impartial third party can facilitate difficult conversations, ensuring that both voices are heard and guiding the conversation towards constructive resolution. This mediation can be particularly vital in high-stakes relationships, where the potential for escalation is heightened.

Ultimately, our goal when addressing conflict is to shift from building walls—impeding communication and disconnecting individuals—to building bridges that cultivate understanding and unity. The very act of choosing to resolve conflicts can lay the

The Power of Words

groundwork for healthier future interactions. As we navigate the shadows of disagreement, we must remain resolute in harnessing the power of our words and actions to transform conflict into an opportunity for growth and development.

In conclusion, conflict does not have to mark the end of a relationship; instead, it can herald its transformation into something deeper and richer. With active listening, honest dialogue, collaboration, accountability, and compassion, we possess the tools to rebuild trust and foster meaningful connections. As we embrace conflict as an opportunity, we learn to create harbours of harmony, where understanding flourishes, relationships deepen, and love prevails.

In Tune with the Divine: God's Word as the Ultimate Guide

Listening for Divine Guidance

In an age characterised by overwhelming noise and constant distractions, the ancient practice of listening—especially for divine guidance—often gets overshadowed. Yet, as people of faith, we are called to navigate our lives with intentionality, seeking the wisdom of God as expressed in Scripture. This journey toward deeper understanding, connection, and fulfilment begins with cultivating the habit of listening for divine guidance through God's Word.

Entering into a space of divine communication requires a willingness to immerse ourselves in the Scriptures. The Bible is not merely a collection of historical texts; it is a living document that breathes the Spirit of God, offering insights and direction for every life circumstance. By engaging with the Word, we not only familiarise ourselves with its content but also position ourselves to receive revelation pertinent to our individual experiences.

Listening to God's Word involves more than reading; it requires a posture of openness and reflection. It means approaching Scripture with the anticipation that God will speak directly to us, illuminating our minds and hearts in profound ways. As we delve into this practice, we must remember that the divine guidance we seek is often accompanied by the still, small voice of the Holy Spirit, leading us gently yet firmly on the paths we are meant to take.

To embark on this enlightening journey, let us first explore how we can effectively prepare ourselves to listen actively and attentively to God's voice through His Word. Creating the right environment is vital in our quest for divine guidance. This environment is not limited to a physical space, but also extends to our mental and emotional states. We should strive for a calm and collected disposition, minimising distractions and centring our thoughts on seeking divine wisdom.

Setting aside designated time for study and prayer can significantly enhance our efforts. Early morning hours, before the hustle and bustle of the day begin, or gentle evenings, when the world is winding down, may serve as opportune moments for communion with God's Word. During these moments, we can read Scripture prayerfully, inviting the Holy Spirit to guide our understanding and to reveal truths that resonate with our lives.

As we read, it is beneficial to approach Scripture with questions that arise from our current circumstances. What are the challenges we face? What decisions loom ahead? Seeking guidance in light of our situations compels us to listen with intention, as our hearts and minds become aligned with the desire to hear God's answers.

An essential practice in listening for divine guidance is meditative reading, often referred to as lectio divina. This ancient practice invites individuals into a process of slow and contemplative engagement with the text. It involves four main steps: reading, reflecting, responding, and resting. The first step, reading, encourages us to allow the words to wash over us, paying attention not just to the content, but also to how it may resonate within our spirits.

Following the initial reading, reflection invites us to ponder questions such as: What words or phrases stand out? Why did they capture my attention? In reflecting, we open ourselves to the possibility of being challenged, encouraged, or reminded of God's faithfulness. It is in this space of contemplation that the Holy Spirit often speaks uniquely to our circumstances, offering the divine guidance we seek.

Next comes the response, where we engage with our discoveries through prayer. This may involve expressing our thoughts, desires, or concerns to God, or simply acknowledging His presence in the revelations we have received from the Word. This dialogue reinforces our connection with God and creates a space for further discovery and guidance.

Lastly, we enter into a time of resting, allowing the insights and revelations to settle within us. This may mean holding our newfound understanding close, integrating it into the fabric of our daily lives, or returning to it in prayer and reflection over time. In resting, we cultivate a posture of trust, believing that God is at work within us, guiding our steps as we navigate our worlds.

As we contemplate listening for divine guidance through Scripture, we discover that God uses various means to communicate with us. While reading can provide clarity, there are moments when God's voice may ring through prayer, worship, or even our interactions with others. Scripture serves as an anchor, always directing our hearts back to the truth and encouraging us to discern the multitude of voices clamouring for our attention.

This brings us to the significance of community in our journey of listening for divine guidance. Engaging with fellow believers provides us with perspectives that enrich our understanding of Scripture. Through conversations, sermons, and study groups, we have the opportunity to glean insight from others' experiences and interpretations, broadening our scope of hearing God's voice.

The Power of Words

In the community, we practice the art of listening not only to God but also to one another. Encouraging conversations can stimulate thoughts and insights that go beyond our initial understanding. As we build one another up, we create an environment conducive to divine communication, where each voice contributes to the larger narrative of faith.

However, it is essential to tread carefully when assessing divine guidance from others. While community can be a powerful resource, we must ultimately return to God's Word for confirmation. As we listen to what others share, we should evaluate their contributions against biblical truths, ensuring that we remain grounded in Scripture amidst varying opinions and advice.

Moreover, our listening practice should be accompanied by a willingness to both follow and act upon divine guidance when it is revealed. Listening without action can lead to stagnation, transforming what could be a vibrant faith journey into one that is merely theoretical. In essence, as we hear God's promptings, we must respond in obedience, trusting that our actions, fuelled by His Word, reflect the divine guidance we have received.

Embracing this principle means cultivating a heart that is willing to respond to what we hear. The question then arises: How do we discern whether it is indeed God's voice leading us, or whether it is simply our desires or fears? This discernment often comes through prayerful reflection, seeking counsel from more experienced believers, and grounding ourselves consistently in Scripture. The more attuned we become to God's Word, the more discerning we will be in our listening.

It is vital to remember that God's guidance is not always immediate or straightforward. There will be moments of silence and seasons of waiting, even as we diligently seek. In these times, patience and perseverance are required. Like a runner who trains over time, we develop endurance as we await answers to our prayers and guidance from the Lord.

Incorporating assiduous prayer into our interactions with God's Word can help bridge the gap during these silent seasons. Instead of rushing to fill the absence with our own conclusions, we are invited to wait expectantly for God's interventions. In doing so, we align our hearts with the truth that, while there may be silence, God hears our pleas and sees our struggles, always working behind the scenes for our benefit.

Ultimately, listening for divine guidance is an intentional journey of faith, inviting us to commune deeply with God as we immerse ourselves in His Word. It is a practice that empowers us to navigate our conversations, interactions, and decisions with heavenly insight, enabling profound connections that reflect His love and grace.

By transforming our approach to Scripture into an active listening exercise, we align ourselves with God's heart, becoming vessels of His guidance in our lives and the lives of others. As we proceed with mindfulness, attentiveness, and diligence, we recognise that each verse carries life, relevance, and the power to positively influence our relationships and experiences.

In this continual quest for divine guidance, we must be patient with ourselves and the process. Listening requires practice, vulnerability, and a deep reliance on the Holy Spirit. Embarking on this journey not only enriches our relationship with God but also reshapes how we communicate with others, illuminating our paths with the brilliance of His light.

As we embrace this sacred calling, may we always remember our intent: to listen for divine guidance, to navigate conversations with grace, and to foster connections that reflect the beautiful tapestry of God's love woven throughout our lives. In doing so, we shall truly harness the power of words as both a means of communion with our Creator and as instruments for expressing His transformative love to a world searching for truth.

Scriptural Insights on Communication

In the tapestry of human relationships, communication serves as a binding thread that weaves individuals together. Our words have the remarkable power to uplift, inspire, and connect us. However, in a world increasingly marked by chaos and discord, believers must turn to sacred wisdom for guidance. The Scriptures offer profound insights into the nature and impact of communication, emphasising the importance of intentionality and grace in our dialogue. This section explores key passages that illuminate the art of communication through a biblical lens.

The significance of our words is established in Proverbs 18:21, which states, 'The tongue has the power of life and death, and those who love it will eat its fruit.' This verse succinctly captures the weight of our utterances; the spoken word holds the potential to create or destroy. It sets the stage for an exploration of how believers can harness this power to cultivate nourishing relationships grounded in faith and love. How we choose to communicate can drastically alter the landscape of our interactions and influence the lives of those around us.

James 1:19 encourages believers to approach conversations with intentionality: 'Everyone should be quick to listen, slow to speak, and slow to become angry.' This Scripture highlights the importance of listening before speaking, a virtue that fosters understanding and minimises conflict. Listening is often an overlooked aspect of communication; however, it lays the groundwork for meaningful dialogue. By prioritising active listening, we honour the perspectives of others and create an atmosphere conducive to open exchange.

Within the realm of communication, it is essential to view our words as offerings that can either build or diminish faith. Ephesians 4:29 instructs, 'Do not let any unwholesome talk come out of your mouths, but only what helps build others up according to their needs, that it may benefit those who listen.' This verse serves as both a challenge and a standard for our speech. It calls on believers to be architects of encouragement, choosing expressions that fortify, rather than weaken, the spirits of those around them. The act of speaking with purpose becomes a sacred responsibility, one that reflects the love and grace of our Creator.

In Matthew 12:34-36, Jesus reminds us of the significance of our words and the heart from which they flow: 'For the mouth speaks what the heart is full of. A good man brings good things out of the good stored up in him, and an evil man brings evil things out of the evil stored up in him. But I tell you that everyone will have to give account on the day of judgment for every empty word they have spoken.' Here, we are challenged not only to examine our words but to assess the condition of our hearts. Our communication is an outward reflection of our internal state; thus, engaging in self-reflection becomes vital for cultivating authentic dialogue. The transformative journey of mindful communication begins with the accountability of our hearts.

Scripture also provides wisdom on how to navigate difficult conversations, further emphasising the importance of grace. In Colossians 4:6, Paul writes, 'Let your conversation be always full of grace, seasoned with salt, so that you may know how to answer everyone.' Grace-laden dialogue invites patience, understanding, and kindness—a necessity when addressing contentious topics. The image of seasoning emphasises that communication should be flavourful and enjoyable, rather than bland and lifeless. A gracious tone transforms dialogue from potential conflict into constructive conversation.

Furthermore, Proverbs 15:1 beautifully emphasises the power of gentle words in conflict resolution: 'A gentle answer turns away wrath, but a harsh word stirs up anger.' This passage serves as a poignant reminder that our tone and demeanour matter just as much as our choice of words. Approaching discussions with gentleness brings clarity and serenity, enabling us to de-escalate tensions while fostering connection. The practice of gentleness echoes the character of Christ, inviting His spirit into our conversations and reflecting His love to others.

In the Sermon on the Mount, found in Matthew 5:23-24, Jesus underscores the heart of communication in the context of reconciliation. He teaches, 'Therefore, if you are offering your gift at the altar and there remember that your brother or sister has something against you, leave your gift there in front of the altar. First, go and be reconciled to them; then come and offer your gift.' This passage highlights the necessity of prioritising relationships and mending rifts over our religious duties. It portrays communication as an avenue to healing, urging believers to approach others with humility and a willingness to reconcile.

As believers engage in the practice of communication, prayer is a crucial part of this process, guiding our words and preparing our hearts. Philippians 4:6 offers a foundational principle: 'Do not be anxious about anything, but in every situation, by prayer and petition, with thanksgiving, present your requests to God.' This exhortation to pray provides insight into grounding our conversations in faith and seeking divine wisdom before engaging with others. By inviting prayer into our communication, we position ourselves to listen more intently and respond thoughtfully.

The Power of Words

Additionally, the wisdom found in Proverbs can offer poignant insights. Proverbs 25:11 declares, 'Like apples of gold in settings of silver is a ruling rightly given.' This metaphor highlights the beauty and value of well-timed, thoughtful communication. The image of precious apples and refined silver captures the exquisite nature of speech that is delivered with intention and wisdom. When we rely on biblical principles, our communication transforms into an elegant expression of our faith.

In our digital age, where communication often occurs through screens and social media platforms, the call for intentionality in words becomes increasingly significant. Ephesians 5:16 reminds us to make the most of every opportunity, declaring, 'Making the most of every opportunity, because the days are evil.' This Scripture transcends the physical realm and extends into our online interactions, inviting us to be vigilant with how we present ourselves and communicate in digital spaces. Each post, comment, and conversation is an opportunity for believers to reflect Christ's love and integrity.

The unity of the body of Christ hinges on effective communication, which helps foster understanding and cohesion among believers. 1 Thessalonians 5:11 commands, 'Therefore encourage one another and build each other up, just as in fact you are doing.' Encouragement through communication creates an environment of support and trust, facilitating spiritual growth within the Christian community. Words can empower fellow believers to embrace their identity in Christ and fulfil their God-given purposes.

In considering the weight of our words, we also remember that each individual carries their unique experiences and stories. Understanding and empathising with others is crucial for effective communication, especially in crafting messages that resonate. Romans 12:15 advises, 'Rejoice with those who rejoice; mourn with those who mourn.' By establishing emotional connections with others, we can tailor our responses to him. This humour serves as an entry point for a deeper connection, allowing us to engage with compassion and authenticity.

Luke 6:45 speaks of the heart's influence on our words, stating, 'A good man brings good things out of the good stored up in his heart, and an evil man brings evil things out of the evil stored up in his heart. For the mouth speaks what the heart is full of.' This scriptural insight reinforces the primary theme that communication is a direct reflection of our inner selves. To foster meaningful dialogue, it is essential to nurture our hearts with truth, love, and grace. Engaging with Scripture regularly ensures that our words emerge from a place of abundant goodness.

As we seek to embody biblical communication principles, we find encouragement in Paul's writings in 2 Timothy 2:24-25: 'And the Lord's servant must not be quarrelsome but kind to everyone, able to teach, not resentful. Opponents must be gently instructed, in the hope that God will grant them repentance, leading them to a knowledge of the truth.' This passage serves as a guide for interacting with individuals who may not share our beliefs. Approaching conversations with kindness and humility may open the door for transformative discussions, creating opportunities for sharing the gospel.

Ultimately, biblical insights on communication call us towards a higher standard. Our words, as instruments of God's love, have the potential to reflect His character to the world. Colossians 3:17 urges believers, 'And whatever you do, whether in word or deed, do it all in the name of the Lord Jesus, giving thanks to God the Father through him.' This verse encapsulates the essence of our communication; our words become acts of worship that offer glory to God.

In conclusion, the Scriptures provide a rich foundation for understanding the nature of communication within the context of faith. The call to intentional, gracious dialogue permeates every aspect of our interactions, from the mundane to the profound. As believers, we are challenged to engage with the world around us intentionally, crafting our words to reflect the heart of Christ. By embedding biblical wisdom into our communication practices, we have the profound responsibility and privilege to shape lives, build communities, and honour our Creator through the power of spoken and written expressions.

As we endeavour to communicate with grace, let us root our conversations in the Word of God, embracing His guidance and reflecting His love. May our words be instruments of healing, connection, and transformation, fulfilling our calling as ambassadors of Christ in a world yearning for authentic voices.

Living Out the Word Daily

In a world filled with noise and distractions, the call to live out God's Word daily can often seem overwhelming. Yet, this very act of integrating divine wisdom into our conversations and interactions holds the key to nurturing our relationships and aligning our lives with heavenly principles. By choosing to embody the teachings of Scripture in our speech, we can transform ordinary moments into powerful encounters with the divine. This subchapter will explore the practical steps we can take to incorporate God's Word into our daily conversations, cultivating an atmosphere of love, grace, and intentionality.

The Power of Words

To begin our journey, it's essential to recognise the significance of living out God's Word. Scripture serves not only as a guide but as a lifeline, directing our hearts and minds toward a higher purpose. Jesus emphasised the importance of abiding in His teachings, indicating that doing so would foster a fruitful life. In John 15:5, He states, 'I am the vine; you are the branches. Whoever abides in me and I in him, he it is that bears much fruit, for apart from me you can do nothing.' This passage highlights that through our relationship with God and by living out His Word, we are enabled to generate positive outcomes in our interactions.

The first step in living out God's Word daily is to immerse ourselves in Scripture. The more we engage with His written Word, the more precise our understanding becomes of how to embody its teachings. One effective way to do this is by establishing a consistent routine of reading and meditating on the Bible. This could occur in the early morning before the day begins, during lunch breaks, or in the evening as a winding-down practice. As we read, let us reflect on the passages and ask ourselves how they apply to our daily lives.

Choosing a reading plan can help focus our engagement with Scripture. Whether we opt for a thematic study, a chronological approach through the Bible, or a book-based approach, having a clear plan helps deepen our understanding. For example, if we focus on the theme of love, passages such as 1 Corinthians 13 and 1 John 4 can provide a solid foundation that can be revisited regularly. This can then translate into our conversation, inspiring us to invoke loving language and intentions.

Moreover, we can enhance our understanding by participating in group Bible studies or discussions. Engaging with others allows for diverse perspectives, woven together by a common desire to know God more intimately. This not only deepens our grasp of His Word, but also cultivates a sense of community—strengthening our relationships through shared exploration. The wisdom shared in a group setting can offer insights that we may not have realised on our own, thus enriching our ability to express these teachings in our daily interactions.

As we cultivate our understanding, the next practical step is to internalise God's Word. This involves committing key verses to memory, allowing them to guide us throughout the day. Scripture memorisation creates an arsenal of truth that we can draw upon in times of need, particularly when we are faced with challenging conversations or conflicts. For instance, remembering James 1:19, which reminds us to be 'quick to hear, slow to speak, slow to anger,' can significantly influence our response to challenging situations.

In addition to memorisation, journaling can serve as a powerful tool for internalising God's Word. Writing down reflections on specific verses or lessons we've learned can help solidify our understanding and provide a record of our spiritual growth. Keeping a journal encourages us to articulate our thoughts, turning them into an active dialogue with God. By documenting our progress, we can revisit these reflections during challenging times, reminding ourselves of the wisdom we aspire to embody.

Embracing God's Word also means living a life of integrity and authenticity. When we are committed to aligning our speech with our faith, we must recognise that our words should reflect our values. James 3:10 states, 'From the same mouth come blessing and cursing. My brothers, these things ought not to be so.' If we aim to express love, kindness, and grace—as instructed in Scripture—we must ensure that our conversations mirror these attributes.

Practising authenticity in communication involves assessing our motives. Before we speak, let us pose questions to ourselves: Are our words intended to uplift? Do they serve to encourage or strengthen another person? Are we reflecting the light of Christ in how we engage? By committing to speak from a place of genuine care, we can create an environment of openness and a deeper connection with others.

The Power of Words

One practical way to achieve this is by developing a habit of asking thoughtful questions. Instead of making assumptions, we can take the time to inquire about others' feelings, experiences, and thoughts. This not only showcases our investment in the relationship but also demonstrates our commitment to embodying the love of Christ in our dialogues.

Another key aspect of living out God's Word daily is incorporating grace into our conversations. Ephesians 4:29 reminds us, 'Let no corrupting talk come out of your mouths, but only such as is good for building up, as fits the occasion, that it may give grace to those who hear.' Grace is about recognising the imperfections in ourselves and others, allowing for open dialogue without judgment. Emphasising grace in our conversations helps to foster a safe space where vulnerability can flourish, encouraging more profound connections.

As we apply grace, let's also remember the importance of forgiveness in our speech. Conflicts are an inevitable part of relationships, yet Scripture teaches us to navigate them with humility and love. Rather than allowing anger or bitterness to poison our interactions, we can choose to communicate our feelings calmly and constructively. Addressing grievances in a manner that reflects our commitment to reconciliation highlights the redemptive nature of God's Word.

In the heat of a disagreement, it may be helpful to pause and pray for guidance, seeking to embody the wisdom of Proverbs 15:1: 'A soft answer turns away wrath, but a harsh word stirs up anger.' By reframing our responses through prayer, we can replace our initial, instinctive reactions with thoughtful, God-honouring replies.

Humility also plays a vital role in our everyday conversations. Acknowledging our limitations and mistakes allows others to feel comfortable doing the same. This requires us to be open and honest about our struggles, thus encouraging authenticity in the relationships around us. By being vulnerable with others about our faith journeys and the challenges we face, we foster a culture of grace and understanding, reminding one another that we are all recipients of God's mercy.

Furthermore, expressing gratitude can significantly enhance our conversations. Cultivating an attitude of thankfulness, as we read in 1 Thessalonians 5:16-18, can transform our dialogue and our hearts. When we choose to acknowledge and celebrate the positives in our relationships and express appreciation for others, we initiate a virtuous cycle of encouragement and uplifting communication.

Incorporating compliments and affirmations into our speech is an excellent way to express gratitude. Let us not shy away from recognising the contributions of those around us, be it through small acts of kindness or significant achievements. By offering sincere words of affirmation, we build up those we care about, reflecting God's love through our praises.

Additionally, amidst our daily conversations, let's remember to share the gospel's hope when appropriate. While building relationships is essential, so is our responsibility to share the transformative power of Jesus Christ. This does not always necessitate grand speeches; often, it can be achieved through simple expressions of our faith and the ways in which God has worked in our lives.

For instance, during a conversation about challenges, gently steering the discussion toward God's faithfulness can kindle hope and uplift spirits. Such moments provide an opportunity for divine planting—cultivating seeds of faith in vulnerable heart spaces. As we weave our testimonies into daily dialogue, we shine the light of Christ in the darkness and encourage others to seek the same purpose.

Living out God's Word convincingly hinges on the discipline of intentionality. By being mindful of our words and actions, we create opportunities to authentically reflect Christ's love. Choosing our words with purpose allows us to uplift and inspire those around us continually. Such intentionality may require conscious effort at first, but it gradually becomes a natural extension of our Christian walk.

To solidify our commitments to living out God's Word, it's helpful to set the intention for each day. As the morning dawns, let's take a brief moment to invite the Holy Spirit into our hearts, asking for guidance in our conversations. Pondering scriptures to meditate on can create a framework for speaking life throughout the day. A single verse to focus on, such as Philippians 4:8—'Finally, brothers, whatever is true, whatever is honourable, whatever is just, whatever is pure, whatever is lovely, whatever is commendable, if there is any excellence, if there is anything worthy of praise, think about these things'—can set the tone for an enriching day of meaningful exchanges.

Furthermore, as we reflect on our days, considering our conversations and interactions can offer profound insight into our communication habits. Taking time for self-examination encourages accountability while creating pathways for growth. Let's ask ourselves, did our words bless others today? Did we embody the principles we wish to live by? This practice of reflection not only reinforces our commitments but also informs our future intentions more effectively.

The Power of Words

Before we conclude this journey into living out God's Word daily, let's consider the profound impact our words can have on our relationships and the world around us. Every interaction presents an opportunity to speak life, peace, and encouragement into those we encounter—friends, family members, colleagues, and even strangers. The fruits of the Spirit—love, joy, peace, patience, kindness, goodness, faithfulness, gentleness, self-control—should manifest in our everyday exchanges.

As we adopt the practice of living out God's Word, we become ambassadors of His message. Our speech has the potential to heal, inspire, and connect individuals to their Creator. The transformation of our conversations opens doors for meaningful relationships founded on the teachings of Christ.

In closing, living out the Word daily is about embracing a lifestyle that commits to speaking authentically, graciously, and lovingly. By immersing ourselves in Scripture, being intentional, and embodying God's principles, we become vessels of His message, nurturing relationships that reflect His divine love. Let each word we speak become a testament to the incredible power of God's grace in our lives, shining brightly into the world around us.

Mirrors of the Soul: Reflecting Love Through Dialogue

Understanding Self through Communication

In our interactions with others, our words can often serve as windows into our very souls. Each phrase and sentence we utter is a reflection of our internal landscape—our beliefs, experiences, values, and desires. Understanding ourselves through communication is not merely about analysing our speech; it is about recognising the profound truth that our dialogues hold. Each conversation, whether casual or deep, provides us with an opportunity to reflect on and unveil our innermost selves.

To embark on this journey of self-discovery through communication, one must be willing to engage in self-reflection exercises that prompt an evaluation of what our words convey about our identities and growth. This process can guide us toward greater self-awareness and transformation, inviting deeper connections with others and with our Creator.

Self-Reflection Exercise 1: Journaling Your Conversations

Consider your recent conversations—those that left you feeling uplifted, those you regret, and those that challenged you. Set a timer for 10 minutes and simply write about one or two key dialogues you've had. Focus on what was said, how you felt during the conversation, and the core themes that emerged.

- What emotions or reactions did your words evoke in others?
- Did any of your statements reflect your true beliefs and values?
- Were there sections where you felt disconnected or misaligned with what you voiced?

As you write, allow yourself to be fully present. Use the act of journaling to excavate the layers of meaning behind your words. What do they reveal about you? How does your communication reflect your understanding of yourself and the world around you?

Often, we may find that the words we choose—or avoid—speak volumes about our internal struggles, our triumphs, and the areas of our lives we may be neglecting or celebrating. By documenting these experiences, we create a mirror through which we can view our evolving identities, recognising patterns that may either affirm our growth or expose areas that require nurturing and attention.

Throughout the process of self-reflection, it's essential to acknowledge how dialogues can be influenced not only by our thoughts but also by our emotions. Consider how the weight of anxiety, joy, sadness, or enthusiasm may colour our speech. The nuances in our dialogues often correlate to the emotional tapestry woven into our identity at that moment.

Self-Reflection Exercise 2: Listen to Your Own Voice

Another powerful way to understand the self through communication is to listen to recordings of your own voice, ideally during conversations where you felt authentic and genuine. Many may feel a tinge of discomfort while hearing themselves speak; however, this exercise encourages you to pay attention to your word choice, tone, and the underlying message of your speech.

- When you listen to yourself, what do you notice?
- Are there recurring phrases or themes that emerge?
- Do you sound confident, passionate, or hesitant?
- What does your voice reveal about your internal state during those conversations?

By actively engaging with your recorded dialogues, you gain insight into how effectively you convey your thoughts and feelings. You may uncover habits in your speech that reflect your emotional landscape, revealing both insecurities and strengths. Pay close attention to any dissonances between your intention and delivery—this gap often provides a vital clue into areas for growth.

Self-Reflection Exercise 3: Seeking Feedback from Trusted Individuals

Often, we cannot see ourselves clearly; our biases or insecurities can cloud our perceptions. Reaching out to close friends, family, or mentors for feedback on your communication style can provide a supportive lens through which you can observe the impact of your dialogue.

Ask them questions like:

- How do you perceive my communication style?
- In what ways do you think my words impact our relationship?
- Have you noticed any patterns in the way I express myself?

Engaging in this exercise invites vulnerability as you open yourself to others' insights. It can also shed light on blind spots you may not have been aware of. This type of authenticity can foster deeper connections and significantly increase your understanding of how your dialogues resonate with those around you.

As you gather feedback, try to approach it with a mindset of growth rather than defensiveness. Recognise that each voice, perception, and observation presents an opportunity to view yourself from a different perspective, allowing you to navigate your self-discovery journey with greater awareness.

The Power of Values in Dialogue

When we consider how dialogues reflect our inner selves, it is crucial to take into account the values that underpin our communication. Our values serve as the compass that directs our words, often contributing to the essence of who we are.

As believers, it is imperative to recognise how our faith shapes and influences our speech. For example, the biblical concept of love acts as a powerful guiding principle. In our words, we can echo the love of God, mirroring His intent to build relationships and foster community. Love, in itself, is a value that cultivates understanding, compassion, and grace—traits that we can choose to embody in our communications.

Engaging in self-reflection around our values prompts us to ask:

- What values are central to our identity?
- How do these values manifest themselves in my speech?
- Are there any misalignments between my communicated values and my true beliefs?

Self-Reflection Exercise 4: Value Mapping

To further explore your values, consider creating a value map. List down your core values—faith, family, honesty, compassion, etc. Reflect on how these values manifest in your dialogues.

For each value, note:

- Examples of conversations you've had where this value was evident.
- Instances where you felt your dialogue didn't align with this value.
- Ways to strengthen the alignment between your values and your words moving forward.

This mapping process provides not only clarity on the values that govern your life but also illuminates the paths where your dialogues can better reflect your true self. We can become more intentional in our speech when we are aware of our values, ultimately leading to more authentic relationships.

Choosing Transformational Language

An essential aspect of understanding oneself through communication is recognising the power of language in shaping our identities. The words we choose can manifest our beliefs and emotions, actively participating in our identity formation. Transformative language holds the potential to heal, uplift, and inspire, while unintentional speech may contribute to dissatisfaction, misunderstanding, and conflict.

Begin to observe how you frame your thoughts. Do your words express hope and positivity, or do they lean toward negativity and self-doubt? Are they affirming your strengths, or are they highlighting shortcomings?

Self-Reflection Exercise 5: Affirmation Practice

Take time each day to practice positive affirmations, speaking them aloud or writing them down. Phrase them in a way that aligns with your values and aspirations. For instance:

- 'I am capable of love and kindness in my interactions.'
- 'I communicate with clarity and intention.'
- 'My words reflect the light of God in my life.'

Through this practice, you will begin to notice how positive language can transform your dialogue and shape your approach to self-expression. As you affirm these truths, you may embody them more fully in your interactions.

Mapping this inward journey encourages us to see language as sacred and transformative. When we view communication as an opportunity to mirror our best selves, we can offer the world not just words, but life.

Understanding Our Growth through Dialogue

In addition to reflecting on who we are, it's essential to recognise how our dialogues can act as indicators of our growth over time. Each conversation can document an evolution in our thoughts, beliefs, and perspectives, allowing us to chart our development and redefine our identities in light of our experiences.

Self-Reflection Exercise 6: The Conversation Timeline

Construct a timeline of significant conversations that have shaped your understanding of yourself over the past year. Identify key phrases or insights that arose during those dialogues that resonated with you.

- How did each conversation contribute to your growth?
- In what ways did your perspectives shift?
- What new ideas or beliefs were introduced?

This timeline will empower you to understand how your dialogues reflect your evolving identity. By examining conversations that sparked change, you can celebrate your growth and commit to embracing further transformation.

The Power of Words

Moreover, these exercises remind us that our communication isn't one-dimensional. The interplay between speech and identity is rich and multifaceted, with both serving as companions in our lifelong journey towards self-understanding and spiritual growth. In this light, open dialogue isn't simply about communicating ideas; it becomes a form of relational art that mirrors the development of our souls.

In this ongoing exploration, one may also feel led to invite God into the conversation, seeking wisdom and clarity through prayer. As we desire to communicate effectively and authentically, turning to Scripture for guidance can reveal profound insights into the heart of communication. Consider the letters of Paul, the parables of Jesus, and the encouragement found in the Psalms, all of which model how our words can pour forth from a wellspring of love and faith.

Self-Reflection Exercise 7: Spirit-Led Conversations

Challenge yourself to engage in one conversation this week with a desire to reflect God's heart.

- Pray before the conversation, seeking guidance for your words and discernment for listening.
- Afterwards, reflect on how this interaction felt:

- Did you notice any changes in your approach?
- How did it impact the other person?

Conversations centred on divine intent will invariably reflect love, compassion, and patience. As our outer dialogues align more closely with godly values, our understanding of ourselves becomes more deeply intertwined with our Creator's heart.

As we conclude this exploration of understanding the self through communication, carry forward the understanding that dialogue is a tool for growth. Our words can illuminate our hearts, reveal our values, and guide us toward transformation. Engage in self-reflection regularly, eager to uncover new dimensions of your identity and embrace the journey ahead. In every dialogue, you have the power to mirror love and grace, fostering deeper relationships that reflect the beauty of your soul—all while walking in alignment with God's truth.

God's Image in Our Words

In a world characterised by a cacophony of voices, we must pause to consider the power of our words and the divine implications they carry. Each utterance we make has the potential to reflect divine love, embody the teachings of our faith, and ultimately reveal the nature of God to those around us. If our dialogues serve as mirrors

The Power of Words

of our innermost selves, what reflections do we project? How do our words depict God's image to the world? These are the questions we must grapple with as we seek to nurture connections grounded in authenticity and spiritual truth.

From a biblical perspective, words are not mere sounds; they are vehicles for divine communication and expressions of our faith. Whether spoken in joy or sorrow, the essence of God's character can often be detected in the way we communicate. The book of Proverbs offers profound wisdom in this area: 'The tongue has the power of life and death, and those who love it will eat its fruits' (Proverbs 18:21, NIV). This statement encapsulates the gravity of our verbal expressions—our words can bring life, healing, encouragement, and hope or decay, disillusionment, and despair. As believers, we are called to elevate our dialogues to reflect the unchanging nature of God, who embodies love, grace, and truth.

Embracing the truth that our dialogues reveal God's love invites us to be more intentional in our speech. When we speak from a place of love and faith, we cultivate an environment ripe for understanding, compassion, and acceptance. In John 13:34-35, Jesus commands us to love one another, stating that the world will know we are His disciples by our love for one another. This love is not hypothetical; it must be expressed through tangible actions, including our words and deeds.

The Power of Words

When we choose to articulate our thoughts in ways that promote unity and understanding, we fulfil our divine purpose of being conduits of God's love. Each time we choose kind words over harsh language, compassion over neglect, we lean into the exemplary nature of Christ. Additionally, our words can hold the potential to build another person up and encourage them in their unique journey, just as God recognises and affirms the intrinsic value and potential within each of us.

Understanding that we are made in the image of God (Genesis 1:26-27) compels us to examine how our verbal exchanges mirror who He is. God's image in us is not intended to be hidden or suppressed but instead manifests in our ability to communicate meaningfully and lovingly. As His image-bearers, we reflect His nature through our interactions, affirming the divine relationship we share with Him and with one another.

As we embark on this exploration of God's image in our words, we must consider the various dimensions of this reflection. Language is multifaceted. It encompasses not only the spoken and written words we exchange but also the tone, emotion, and intent behind them. Collectively, these elements create a tapestry of communication that either points toward the divine or detracts from it. By being attuned to this phenomenon, we can train ourselves to be more mindful of our speech, ensuring it aligns with the love and guidance of our Creator.

To further delve into the theological significance of our words, we observe that Jesus, the Word made flesh (John 1:14), exemplified the profound connection between divine communication and human interaction. His life was a testament to the power of spoken truth, healing, and encouragement. Not only did His words instruct, but they also transformed lives. When He spoke to the weary, the afflicted, or the ostracised, He infused hope, affording dignity and worth to those often disregarded by society. His divinely inspired dialogues exemplify how our communication should uplift, heal, and speak life into others.

This notion of embodying God's image through our words aligns with the call to live out the truth we find in Scripture. Ephesians 4:29 admonishes us, 'Do not let any unwholesome talk come out of your mouths, but only what helps build others up according to their needs, that it may benefit those who listen.' Such instruction encourages us to engage in speaking words that are beneficial actively. The challenge lies in our ability to discern the unique needs of each person we encounter, thus positioning our words as vessels of divine love that resonate with their circumstances.

The Power of Words

Practically, reflecting God's love in our conversations requires vulnerability. To ensure our dialogues embody authenticity, we must be willing to engage in meaningful exchanges that may challenge our comfort zones. Jesus modelled this vulnerability throughout His ministry, as He dined with sinners and was involved with questions arising from doubt, fear, and uncertainty. By inviting others into open dialogue, He not only communicated love but also established deeper relationships rooted in mutual respect and understanding.

The power of vulnerability in our conversations fosters an environment where others feel safe expressing their true selves. When we approach dialogue without pretence, our authentic expressions resonate with God's grace. It is indeed through our willingness to share our journeys with honesty that we foster community—one where authentic love proliferates. Such interactions remind those around us that they are valued, worthy of connection, and deserving of our compassionate engagement.

The image of God within us reflects not only His love but also His creativity. Our words can paint beautiful narratives, sharing visions filled with hope and transformation. They can inspire action and incite enthusiasm, prompting others to dream, engage, and dare to step into the unknown, all grounded in faith. Consider the narratives woven by biblical figures who spoke forth visions and

The Power of Words

dreams that shaped the trajectory of their communities. Their words catalysed actions and sparked movements that echoed God's heart for His people.

The act of speaking life is inherently powerful; it can unlock potential, not just in the words' listeners but also in the speaker themselves. When we offer encouragement, affirmation, or even a simple acknowledgement of someone's worth, we become participants in something divine—a reflection of God's love—inviting the fullness of Scripture into our conversations. Language thus transforms from mere communication into a divine instrument capable of wielding influence over circumstances and lives.

Moreover, our dialogues reveal our growth as individuals. As we communicate with others, we often encounter opportunities for self-reflection. Are our words affirming the value of others? Are they enhancing our relationships? Do we consider the feelings and perspectives of those we interact with? Engaging in such introspection strengthens our resolve to speak truthfully, graciously, and as bearers of divine light. As we grow more attuned to God's image in us, our dialogues naturally become richer, more layered, and beautifully reflective of His love.

Conversely, we must also acknowledge the pitfalls of our speech. Words can harm—to scar, to alienate, and to demean. The biblical admonishments against gossip and slander remind us that, too often, the intensity of our frustration, anger, or disappointment can seep into our communications with others, distorting our reflections of God's love. Recognising that our dialogues can sometimes turn away from grace is an essential aspect of our spiritual growth. By taking accountability for these moments, we can recalibrate our expressions and generate dialogues centred on heart and healing.

A challenging yet transformative process lies in learning how to reconcile our shortcomings. Honesty and confession pave the way for healing conversations, allowing both parties to navigate through misunderstandings with humility. By approaching dialogues in this way, we mirror God's understanding and grace, which transcends our failures and provides opportunities for redemption and restoration.

Awareness of our linguistic power should encourage us to avoid engaging in trivial conversations or thoughtless exchanges. Instead, we ought to invest in cultivating dialogues that echo God's love and serve a greater purpose. With this perspective, we begin to reframe our conversations. We see our words not just as tools of expression but as extensions of our faith and our relationship with God. We begin to ask ourselves guiding questions: Am I sharing words that build faith and incite love? Am I inviting God's presence into my dialogues? Are the exchanges I have aligned with the teachings of Christ? By consistently asking these questions, we deepen our connection to the divine and one another.

Embracing this journey is neither a superficial nor instantaneous endeavour; instead, it involves sustained effort, introspection, and a commitment to lifelong growth. Each conversation presents an opportunity to reflect God's love more profoundly in an ever-changing world. The tapestry of our interactions can either illustrate an image of discord or depict a portrait of divine unity. When we lean into the grace afforded to us as we navigate this journey, we allow God's image to radiate through our words, establishing a legacy of love that reverberates far beyond us.

Thus, let us begin each day with a commitment to communicate with purpose, ensuring that every word holds the power to uplift and unite. Our challenges, doubts, victories, and joys should weave together to create a narrative reflective of God's image, urging us and others toward understanding, acceptance, and love.

As we embody the essence of divine love through our speeches, we have the privilege of participating in God's mission. This mission seeks to heal the broken and foster community among believers. May we endeavour to cultivate our words with intention, creating a transformative dialogue that resonates with the profound love of our Creator. Each conversation becomes an act of worship, recognising the marvellous image of God within ourselves and others, ultimately painting breathtaking pictures of grace in our shared humanity.

Cultivating Relationships Through Love

In a world that often feels divided and contentious, the ability to cultivate relationships through love becomes not just a cherished aspiration but a divine calling. At the heart of our interactions lies a profound truth: the words we choose have the potential to either build bridges or erect walls. As we explore how dialogue can be a vehicle for reflecting God's love, we will delve into practical applications and actionable steps that can transform our conversations into acts of love. Through intentional communication, we can create environments that nurture connections and foster enduring bonds, promoting a harmonious atmosphere that celebrates the divine essence within each of us.

To begin with, we must recognise that love isn't merely an abstract emotion; it is an active choice we make, especially in our dialogues. The beauty of communicating love lies in its simplicity—each encouraging word, every thoughtful inquiry, and all instances of patient listening can become loving acts when grounded in sincerity and faith. By embracing the principles of love in our conversations, we can emulate Christ's message of compassion and grace, allowing our words to serve as channels through which His love flows into the lives of others.

One of the foundational elements of speaking love involves our intent. When we approach dialogue to reflect God's love, our mindset shifts. We begin to see conversations not simply as exchanges of information but as opportunities to uplift and compassionately connect with others. The first step in cultivating relationships through love is setting this intention firmly in our hearts.

A practical way to harness this loving intent is to start each conversation with a prayer. Inviting God into our interactions clears our minds of distractions and floods our hearts with His love. For instance, before engaging in a difficult conversation, whether with a colleague, a family member, or even a stranger, taking a moment to pause and pray for guidance can profoundly impact the tone of the dialogue. By asking God for wisdom, we allow Him to direct our words, infusing them with grace and empathy.

Once we establish love as our foundational intent, we can explore how to express it through our dialogue. Here are several practical strategies to ensure our conversations reflect love:

1. Affirmative Language:

One of the most powerful tools in our communication arsenal is affirmative language. Choosing to emphasise positive aspects during conversations not only uplifts the recipient but also fosters a more constructive atmosphere. Instead of pointing out flaws or mistakes, we can pivot the conversation towards strengths and potential.

For example, in a work setting, rather than simply criticising a colleague's approach on a project, we might say, 'I really appreciate your creativity in tackling this issue. Have you thought about how we might build on that idea?' This method nurtures a supportive dialogue that reflects love and encourages collaboration.

2. Active Listening:

Listening is an essential yet often overlooked aspect of loving dialogue. Through active listening, we validate the speaker's feelings, creating a space where they feel heard and understood. This practice reminds us that love is not only about speaking but also about grasping the hearts of others in our conversations.

In a recent discussion with a friend who was facing a challenging situation, instead of jumping in with advice, I consciously practised active listening. I maintained eye contact, nodded in understanding, and repeated back what they had shared. By reflecting their words, I demonstrated that their feelings were significant and worthy of my time.

3. Questioning with Grace:

When we ask questions in conversations, they should arise from genuine curiosity and care rather than interrogation. Framing our questions thoughtfully encourages openness and reveals our willingness to connect.

Consider how we phrase inquiries. Instead of asking, 'Why didn't you do it this way?' we might rephrase to, 'What were the thoughts behind your decision?' This slight shift in language embodies love and respect, inviting a deeper connection instead of creating defensiveness.

4. Expressing Gratitude:

Gratitude is a love language that can transform our interactions. Taking the time to express appreciation for others not only enriches our relationships but reflects God's love back onto them.

Whether it's acknowledging someone for their hard work or simply thanking a friend for their support, these expressions cultivate a warm environment. For instance, sending a handwritten note to thank someone after a shared experience can deepen the relationship, reinforcing that they matter to you.

5. *Practising Empathy:*

Empathy is the ability to understand and share the feelings of another. It's a critical skill in fostering loving dialogues. When we empathise, our words become infused with understanding, allowing us to connect not just at a surface level, but in a more profound and heartfelt way.

To practice empathy, we pause before responding to someone's news and ask ourselves how we would feel if we were in their shoes. If I hear a colleague share their struggles with balancing work and family life, rather than simply offering platitudes, I could respond with, 'I can only imagine how overwhelming that feels. I admire how you're managing everything.' This response validates their feelings and promotes love through understanding.

6. *Being Mindful of Timing:*

Timing can play a crucial role in the effectiveness of our words. Speaking love doesn't always mean addressing something immediately; sometimes, a little space allows for healing or reflection. We must recognise when it's appropriate to step back and wait for better moments to address sensitive topics.

The Power of Words

One lesson came from a personal experience where the urgency to resolve conflict overshadowed the need for compassion. I rushed to address grievances with a friend during a tense moment, only to have the conversation escalate. Later, I discovered that setting a time to talk when emotions had settled led to a more productive and loving dialogue.

7. Sharing Personal Stories:

Stories have a remarkable ability to bridge gaps between souls. Sharing personal experiences, especially those that reveal vulnerability, can foster deeper connections. When we reveal ourselves, we invite others to do the same, which nurtures mutual understanding and love.

For instance, during a gathering, I shared a moment of struggle I faced while raising my children. Others began to share their stories, evoking laughter, tears, and a shared resonance with life's challenges. This exchange not only formed solidarity among us but also epitomised love through shared experiences.

8. Choosing Nonviolent Communication:

Nonviolent Communication (NVC) is an approach that fosters positive interactions free from blame, criticism, or judgment—elements that can disrupt love. By following NVC principles, we can articulate our feelings and needs while simultaneously honouring the other person's humanity.

For instance, instead of stating, 'You always misunderstand me,' one could express, 'I feel hurt when my words seem misinterpreted; could we explore how we might communicate more effectively?' This approach opens up paths to dialogue founded on love and respect.

9. Celebrating Others:

Love blooms in environments where people feel celebrated. Acknowledging achievement, no matter how small, nurtures relationships. We must look for opportunities to honour our loved ones—be it a milestone at work or a personal triumph. Sharing these moments nurtures a sense of belonging and love.

One effective practice could be initiating a monthly dinner where each person shares their highlights or victories from the past month. Such initiatives transform relationships, creating a collective atmosphere of mutual encouragement and love.

10. Being Consistent:

Finally, love in dialogue must be consistent. Our words, intentions, and actions must align over time. Inconsistent communication, such as saying loving things one day and being dismissive the next, can confuse and hurt those around you.

Developing loving dialogue is a journey that requires practice, self-awareness, and commitment. Much like nurturing a garden, it demands patience and dedication. By tending to our words and being intentional in our communication, we cultivate not only loving relationships but also a deeper alignment with God's love.

In our quest to reflect God's love through dialogue, we are also called to evaluate the fruit of our words consistently. Are they producing kindness and understanding, or are they sowing discord and isolation? This ongoing reflection can serve as a spiritual exercise, deepening our relationship with God as we seek His guidance in our conversations.

Moreover, let us not forget the immense power of adaptability. Engaging in conversations with a spirit of love might require us to be open to change, to evolve our ways of speaking, and even to revisit past dialogues that may not have reflected the love of Christ.

In practical terms, creating a community rooted in love begins with each of us. When we engage with sincerity and intention, we not only impact our relationships but also create a ripple effect within our communities. Conversations infused with love become a source of healing not just for ourselves but also for others, drawing them closer to God's grace.

As we cultivate relationships through love, let's celebrate the beauty of connection that follows. The reality is that every word we speak can either dampen or uplift a spirit—words can bring hope and restore joy. By creating opportunities to express love through our conversations with intention, we become bearers of light, illuminating paths for those around us.

In conclusion, the art of cultivating relationships through love is both a sacred responsibility and a treasured opportunity. It invites us into a deeper understanding of how God's love can be communicated through our everyday interactions. Each tip illustrated serves as a reminder that love is not merely something we say, but something we actively embody through our words and actions. By harnessing the transformative power of loving dialogue, we nourish our relationships, reflect God's love, and contribute to a world that so desperately needs the unifying force of kindness and grace.

May we stand firm in our commitment to be conduits of love, ensuring our dialogues are expressions of God's heart at every turn. As we step forth into our conversations, let us embody the love we

The Power of Words

wish to share, leaving our hearts and the hearts of those we encounter forever touched by the beauty of divine communication.

A Journey Beyond Words: Feelings and the Art of Listening

The Landscape of Listening

In our fast-paced world, the art of listening is often overshadowed by the noise of daily life. It's too easy to become distracted by the myriad of stimuli that vie for our attention, leading to conversations that flounder rather than flourish. Yet, deep within the intricacies of our interactions lies a transformative power—the power of listening. True listening goes beyond simply hearing sounds; it requires an earnest engagement with the speaker, fostering connection and understanding that can greatly enrich our relationships.

Listening is an act of love; it signals to the speaker that their thoughts and feelings are valued. When we genuinely listen, we open the door to empathy and unity, bridging the gaps that can form between us. As we venture into this vivid landscape of listening, it is essential to appreciate its depth and complexity. In this subchapter, we will explore the key components of active listening, unpacking how these elements contribute to meaningful dialogue and transformative relationships.

The Essence of Listening

Before delving into the mechanics of active listening, it's essential to understand its essence. Listening is an intentional process rooted in the desire to understand rather than merely respond. In a culture where opinions can be vocalised loudly and rapidly, many people listen primarily to formulate their replies. Instead, active listening entails immersing ourselves in the speaker's perspective and interpretation.

This deeper level of engagement creates a space for the speaker to express themselves authentically. When individuals feel heard, it affirms their worth and opens pathways for deeper communication. This acknowledgement of one another can embody God's love and grace, creating an environment ripe for transformation and healing. When we listen actively, we invite people into a dialogue where they can share their struggles, joys, and hopes without fear of judgment or interruption.

Components of Active Listening

To flesh out the art of listening, let's dissect its essential components:

1. Full Attention

True listening begins with full attention. In a world teeming with distractions, focusing entirely on the speaker is a profound act of respect. This means putting away our devices, silencing internal dialogues, and blocking out external noise. By committing our attention, we signal to the speaker that their words are significant. This can be enhanced by using nonverbal cues such as nodding, maintaining eye contact, and leaning forward slightly, which all convey engagement.

2. Empathy

Empathy—the ability to put ourselves in someone else's shoes—is a cornerstone of effective listening. As we attentively listen, we ask ourselves what the speaker might be feeling and how their experiences shape their perspective. By nurturing empathy, we honour the emotions embedded in their communication. Responding with phrases like, 'I can see this is really important to you,' fosters a deeper connection, allowing the speaker to feel understood and validated.

3. Clarification

After grasping the overall message, the next step in active listening involves seeking clarification. This involves asking open-ended questions that encourage the speaker to provide more detailed

The Power of Words

insight. Questions such as, 'What do you mean when you say...?' or 'How did that make you feel?' invite elaboration and create space for deeper exploration. This process not only enhances understanding but also reinforces our interest in their experiences.

4. Reflection

Reflecting on what we've heard is another critical component of active listening. Paraphrasing the speaker's words shows that we are actively processing their message. This might involve stating, 'It sounds like you're saying that...' or 'What I hear you describing is...' Such reflections help clarify any miscommunication while allowing the speaker to confirm or expand upon their thoughts. This process can also illuminate feelings that may not have been initially articulated.

5. Nonverbal Communication

Listening is not solely a verbal exchange; nonverbal cues strengthen the message being conveyed. Our body language, posture, and tone of voice play significant roles in communicating attentiveness and understanding. A relaxed posture, warm expressions, and soft voice tones can communicate safety and encouragement, inviting deeper sharing. Adapting our body language to reflect engagement fosters a supportive environment and complements the words being exchanged.

6. Patience

Active listening also requires patience; it's about allowing the speaker the time they need to articulate their thoughts and feelings. In moments of silence, we might feel the urge to fill the void with our own words, but it is in these pauses that introspection often occurs. Giving someone the necessary time to gather their thoughts or process their feelings can lead to richer conversations, as it allows for authentic expression without the pressure of rushing.

7. Avoiding Judgment

An essential aspect of active listening is the commitment to suspend judgment. Often, the instinct to evaluate or critique the speaker's sentiments can inhibit genuine understanding. Listening without bias fosters an environment where individuals feel secure enough to express their vulnerabilities. We can cultivate this non-judgmental stance by reminding ourselves that everyone's experiences and feelings are valid, regardless of whether we agree with them or not.

8. Responding Constructively

Finally, active listening culminates in constructive responses. After fully engaging with the speaker's narrative, we can offer our thoughts, support, or feedback based on what we've learned. These responses can reinforce feelings of connection and validation.

Encouraging phrases like, 'Thank you for sharing that with me—how can I support you further?' serve as bridges that deepen relational bonds.

Challenges to Active Listening

While active listening is an invaluable skill, it does come with challenges. In our culture of instantaneous communication and busy lifestyles, distractions abound. Often, we find ourselves preoccupied with personal concerns, making it difficult to remain present in conversations. Recognising these barriers is the first step towards overcoming them.

Another challenge is the discomfort that may arise when listening to conversations laden with conflict or emotion. These discussions can elicit fear or defensiveness, leading us to disengage or interject prematurely. Practising mindfulness can help counter these reactions—by being aware of our triggers and responses, we can better manage our instincts, allowing us to remain grounded in the conversation.

Cultivating the Art of Listening

To enrich our listening skills, intentional practice is crucial. Like any other discipline, the art of listening requires consistent effort and dedication. Here are some strategies to cultivate this essential skill:

Practice Mindfulness

Developing mindfulness is an excellent foundation for enhancing listening skills. Mindfulness exercises—such as focused breathing or meditative practices—can help us cultivate presence. This presence not only heightens our awareness of distractions but also enriches our interactions with others.

Set Intentions

Before engaging in conversations, approach them to listen deeply. Setting goals to stay present, avoid interruptions, and validate the speaker's feelings can help reframe our mindset. By consciously prioritising listening, we pave the way for transformative dialogues.

Engage in Role-Playing

Practising active listening in controlled settings—such as workshops or role-playing exercises—can build confidence in applying these skills. Engaging with different perspectives broadens our understanding and prepares us for real-life situations.

Seek Feedback

After engaging in conversations, solicit feedback from the speaker about your listening effectiveness. Inquire about specific moments they felt understood or validated, as well as areas where you could improve. This feedback loop enhances growth and offers tangible insights into your communicative habits.

Limit Multitasking

To enhance listening skills, commit to minimising distractions during conversations. Limiting technology and external stimuli allows us to give our full attention. Practising living fully in the moment helps us embrace authenticity in our dialogues.

In this journey to develop the art of listening, we must also embrace vulnerability. Acknowledging our imperfections enables us to connect with others on a deeper level. By acknowledging when we struggle to listen or express ourselves, we can foster an environment of understanding and compassion.

The Transformative Power of Listening

Listening is not just a skill; it is a catalyst for transformation. Throughout our lives, the relationships we nourish can significantly impact our personal growth and emotional well-being. Genuine listening inspires dialogue that fosters connections, helping individuals feel seen, heard, and valued.

As we transform our listening practices, we begin to witness the ripple effects in our relationships. Families become united through understanding, friendships deepen with authenticity, and community bonds strengthen through compassion. The art of listening can inspire healing, fostering an atmosphere where grace and love flourish.

Furthermore, listening nurtures our spiritual growth. In the context of faith, listening to others becomes a pathway to understanding God's heart. As we hear the experiences and struggles of our brothers and sisters, we become more acutely aware of God's presence in their lives. The act of listening becomes a means of divine communication, helping us grow in our faith and empathy.

In a world that often prioritises speaking, let us remember that listening is equally vital. It holds the keys to understanding, healing, and transformation in relationships, offering us a glimpse into the heart of our fellow travellers on this earthly journey. Through this art, we can respond to God's call to love our neighbours as ourselves, co-creating conversations that echo His grace.

As we continue to practice the art of listening, may we be inspired to amplify its impact. Let's encourage others to join us on this journey, reminding them of the power found within their words and the healing that can arise when we simply choose to listen. In doing so, we become conduits of love, building bridges over the landscape of our relationships—bridges that carry hope, understanding, and connection.

Empathy: The Heart of Listening

In the intricate dance of communication, empathy serves as the rhythm guiding each interaction. It is not merely about understanding the words spoken; it is about grasping the essence of what lies beneath them. To listen with empathy is to engage fully with another person's experience and emotions, fostering deeper connections that transcend the surface of conversation. In this subchapter, we will delve into the art of empathetic listening, examining how it can foster bonds of trust, mutual understanding, and love—qualities essential for nurturing godly relationships.

Listening is often perceived as a passive act, yet when infused with empathy, it becomes a dynamic force that can transform conversations and relationships. Empathy allows us to connect with others on a profound level, enabling us to comprehend their feelings, thoughts, and needs. It urges us to prioritise the emotional landscape of our dialogues, enriching our interactions with authenticity and grace.

At its core, empathy involves stepping into someone else's shoes, viewing the world from their perspective. It requires a willingness to acknowledge their feelings without judgment, creating a safe space for open communication. This is particularly important in a faith-based context, where love and acceptance are at the heart of our interactions.

The Power of Words

When we listen with empathy, we become more adept at identifying the nonverbal cues that often accompany spoken words. A sigh, a shift in posture, or a fleeting glance can convey volumes about a person's emotional state. By honing our sensitivity to these signals, we open ourselves up to a richer understanding of the messages being communicated. Nonverbal cues often reflect what words cannot express, making them a vital aspect of empathetic listening.

Consider a time when someone shared a struggle with you. Perhaps they were grappling with feelings of inadequacy or fear. While their words communicated their distress, it was likely their body language—slumped shoulders, downcast eyes, or a quivering voice—that truly conveyed the depth of their pain. As a listener, when you attuned yourself to these subtle cues, you were empowered to respond in a way that acknowledged their emotional reality.

Empathy invites us to not only hear but also to feel. This deeper listening fosters trust, as it assures the speaker that they are seen and understood. Trust is a foundational component of any meaningful relationship, and it is cultivated through the consistent practice of empathetic listening. When others feel that their emotions are validated, they are more likely to share openly, contributing to a cycle of communication characterised by transparency and love.

The power of empathy in listening extends beyond individual relationships; it can transform entire communities. When empathy becomes the cornerstone of communication, it creates an environment where individuals feel secure enough to express their vulnerabilities. In a world often rife with judgment and misunderstanding, such environments can serve as havens for healing and growth. Communities built on empathetic communication flourish, as members support one another emotionally and spiritually, reflecting the love of Christ in their interactions.

Biblically, we see numerous examples of empathetic listening that resonate with the teachings of Jesus. In John 11, when Jesus was confronted with Lazarus' death, He responded not with immediate action but with profound empathy. He wept alongside Mary and Martha, sharing in their sorrow before bringing Lazarus back to life. His tears demonstrated that empathy is not about having the right answers or solutions; it is about being present and acknowledging the feelings of others.

Empathy invites us to embrace vulnerability in our interactions. In moments where we truly listen to another's pain, we often become emotionally affected ourselves. This sharing of human experience can foster deeper connections, as it invites both parties to explore their feelings authentically and openly. Vulnerability allows us to connect the threads of our lives, weaving a tapestry of shared experiences that fortify our relationships.

To engage in empathetic listening, we must cultivate an open-minded mindset. This involves setting aside distractions and fully investing our attention in the person speaking. When we actively listen—making eye contact, nodding, and responding appropriately—we signal that we are both physically and emotionally present. The act of being physically present is crucial, as it lays the groundwork for emotional connection.

However, empathetic listening goes beyond engagement—it requires patience and understanding. Sometimes, individuals may not immediately articulate their thoughts or feelings clearly. They may take their time to gather their thoughts or need reassurance that it is safe to express themselves. In such moments, it is our role as empathetic listeners to hold space, allowing silence to feel comfortable and nurturing.

Silence, when embraced in a conversation, can be a powerful tool. It allows both the speaker and the listener to absorb what has been shared, creating a reflective pause where emotions and thoughts can settle. This silence invites contemplation and signals to the speaker that their words are valued, encouraging them to continue sharing as they feel ready. Empathy flourishes in these moments when we resist the urge to fill silence with our voices and instead allow the other person to gather their thoughts.

Moreover, empathy encourages us to respond thoughtfully and compassionately. When someone confides their troubles in us, our responses should reflect an understanding of their experience rather than jumping to solutions or judgment. It can be immensely powerful to simply acknowledge their feelings, saying something like, 'That sounds incredibly difficult; I'm sorry you're going through this.' Such a response validates their experience and reinforces the bond of trust between speaker and listener.

In nurturing empathetic listening, we should remember that our tone of voice and body language play pivotal roles in how our words are received. A warm tone and open posture can convey support and acceptance, while a dismissive tone or closed stance can alienate even the most well-intentioned response. When we align our verbal expressions with our nonverbal ones, we create a harmonious message characterised by love and understanding—a fundamental aspect of building godly relationships.

The power of empathy extends beyond personal interactions; it redefines entire communities. An empathetic approach to listening can bridge divides, fostering inclusivity in spaces where differing viewpoints exist. In family gatherings, workplaces, and faith communities, empathetic listening encourages dialogues that acknowledge and honour diverse perspectives, promoting understanding rather than discord.

As we cultivate empathy in our lives, we start to see its ripple effects. Imagine a scenario where one individual responds empathetically to a friend's struggles. That friend, feeling heard and validated, may be inspired to pay this kindness forward by engaging empathetically with another person in need. This chain reaction of empathy creates a nurturing environment, enriching relationships among all involved.

In faith communities, this ripple effect is crucial. When individuals embody the principles of empathetic listening, they reflect Christ's love in their interactions with others. They become conduits of grace, fostering connections that uplift and support everyone around them. Such environments encourage believers to share their burdens, reminding each other of the promise found in Galatians 6:2: 'Carry each other's burdens, and in this way, you will fulfil the law of Christ.'

As we strive to embody empathy in our conversations, it is essential to reflect on our intentions. What motivates us to listen? Do we seek to genuinely understand the other person's experience, or are we more focused on forming our responses? Being aware of our motivations can foster a deeper commitment to empathetic listening.

To further enhance our empathetic listening skills, we can implement practical techniques that promote effective communication. One such practice is engaging in active listening exercises. These exercises challenge us to avoid interrupting or formulating responses while the other person is speaking. Instead, we can practice summarising what they've shared to ensure we've captured their message accurately. This not only deepens our understanding but also signals to the speaker that their thoughts are worthy of reflection.

Another technique is to explore and express our feelings in response to others' experiences. Sharing our vulnerabilities can foster reciprocity, paving the way for mutual understanding. For example, if a friend shares their struggles with anxiety, we might share a moment when we encountered similar feelings. This openness can foster connection, as it reinforces the notion that we are all human, each navigating our challenges.

Additionally, we can cultivate our awareness of nonverbal cues. Practising mindfulness enhances our ability to tune into the emotions expressed through body language. For instance, while listening, we can pay attention not just to the words spoken but also to the surrounding silence, the gestures made, and the expressions on the speaker's face. By allowing our empathy to guide us, we can respond in ways that honour both their verbal and nonverbal communications.

It is essential to continue nurturing our emotional intelligence. Recognising our emotions equips us to respond empathetically to others. By understanding our feelings, we become more attuned to the emotions of those around us. Emotional intelligence fosters connection, helping us weave empathy into our relationships more seamlessly.

In conclusion, empathy serves as the heart of listening, breathing life into our conversations and nurturing the bonds that define our relationships. By embracing empathetic listening, we can cultivate deeper connections, understanding and love in a world that often prioritises surface-level dialogue. The silent strength of nonverbal cues, coupled with intentional engagement, becomes a transformative force in our interactions.

As we reflect on our journeys, let us commit to embodying empathy in our conversations. Let us set aside distractions, hone our listening skills, and approach every dialogue with a heart open to understanding. By doing so, we become vessels of God's love, fostering environments where grace, compassion, and connection flourish. In this sacred dance of dialogue, may we learn to listen not just with our ears, but with our hearts, recognising the profound power found in every exchange.

Engaging in Communion

Engaging in communion through listening is an art that requires intention, presence, and the willingness to connect beyond mere words. Often, we find ourselves in conversations where the focus is solely on what we will say next, rather than fully immersing ourselves in the moment. This subchapter aims to shift our perspective from being passive participants to active communicators who listen with their hearts, fostering an environment of genuine understanding and authenticity.

At its core, communion is about connection. It is about sharing not just words, but emotions, thoughts, and experiences in a manner that transcends ordinary dialogue. When we listen deeply, we invite the other person into a shared space of vulnerability and openness. This is where relationships are nurtured and bonds are fortified.

To engage in genuine communion, we must first recognise the importance of presence. In a world filled with noise and distraction, dedicating our full attention to another person is a powerful act. It conveys respect, value, and love. The act of being present involves more than just hearing the words spoken; it encompasses observing body language, noticing tone, and understanding the unspoken communication that often carries the heaviest weight.

Before we can engage in communion, we need to cultivate the ability to listen actively. Active listening is not just about nodding along or waiting for our turn to speak; it requires us to focus intently on the speaker. We must set aside our preconceived notions and judgments, entering the conversation with a clean slate. This means putting away our devices, closing our minds to distractions, and truly immersing ourselves in the dialogue.

Active listening begins with physical cues. Making eye contact is crucial; it signals to the speaker that we are engaged in their message. Our body language should also reflect our attentiveness; leaning slightly forward, nodding in affirmation, and maintaining an open stance all contribute to an atmosphere of receptivity. These nonverbal cues create a safe space where the speaker feels valued and understood.

However, listening is not just a physical act; it is an emotional one. We must also strive to connect on a deeper emotional level. This involves empathising with the speaker, attempting to understand their feelings and perspectives. Empathy enables us to relate to the speaker's experiences and to approach the conversation with compassion. When we listen with empathy, we create opportunities for shared healing and support.

As we engage in communion through listening, we can utilise the power of reflection. Reflective listening involves paraphrasing or summarising what the speaker has shared to ensure understanding. This technique not only demonstrates active engagement but also allows the speaker to feel heard. For example, upon hearing someone express frustration about a situation, a reflective listener might respond with, 'It sounds like you're feeling overwhelmed right now.' This validates the speaker's feelings and encourages them to explore their experience further.

Moreover, we must also be mindful of our responses. In conversations, it is easy to fall into the trap of offering advice or solutions before fully understanding the other person's perspective. While our intentions may be rooted in care, jumping to conclusions can inadvertently undermine the importance of the speaker's feelings. Instead, when our responses are grounded in empathy and curiosity, they foster an environment where deeper communion can occur.

To illustrate the transformative power of active communion through listening, let us consider a scenario. Imagine a friend comes to us, visibly upset after receiving criticism at work. If we respond with immediate solutions, we may inadvertently shut down communication. However, if we take the time to listen actively—avoiding interruptions, offering empathetic affirmations, and reflecting their feelings—we create a foundation for deeper understanding. As our friend feels more comfortable sharing, they may speak not only about the incident but also about underlying insecurities or fears, leading to a more profound exchange than we might have anticipated.

The Power of Words

This process of engaging in communion requires patience and perseverance. In our fast-paced world, we may feel compelled to rush through conversations or focus on our agendas. Yet, true communion demands that we anchor ourselves in each moment, valuing the quality of dialogue over the quantity. We must remind ourselves that every conversation is an opportunity for connection and growth. Each time we create a space for honest dialogue, we are sowing the seeds of stronger relationships founded on understanding and respect.

Another essential dimension of engaging in communion through listening is our willingness to embrace vulnerability. Both parties must be open to sharing their truths, fears, and hopes without the fear of judgment. It requires courage to express our innermost thoughts, but when we do so in a safe environment, we strengthen our relational fabric. Vulnerability fosters trust, encourages authenticity, and invites others to share more deeply.

To cultivate this atmosphere, we can begin by sharing our experiences. By modelling vulnerability, we pave the way for others to open up. When we disclose our fears or uncertainties, we signal to our conversation partners that it is safe to explore their feelings without fear of reproach. This mutual exchange enhances the communion experience, creating a tapestry of shared understanding and support.

Furthermore, harnessing patience in our communion can be revitalising. Understand that speaking and listening are not merely transactional; they embody deeper meanings. We must be prepared for moments of silence or introspection, allowing both ourselves and the speaker to process thoughts without rushing toward distraction. Silence is often filled with the essence of communion; it holds space for thoughts to mature and deepen the bond between communicators.

The context in which we engage in communion is equally vital. Our surroundings can influence the quality of our interactions. Creating an environment that encourages openness requires thoughtful consideration. Whether at home, in a coffee shop, or during a casual stroll, the setting can either enhance or hinder the process of communion. We must choose environments that promote relaxation and focus, free from chaos and interruption.

Let's consider the concept of communion in a practical light. It is not merely for large discussions; it extends to everyday interactions. Engaging in communion can be as simple as a conversation with a colleague, a heartfelt exchange with a family member, or even an honest dialogue with ourselves. Each of these moments carries potential for connection and understanding.

The art of listening extends beyond words; it is also accentuated by non-verbal communication. Our facial expressions, gestures, and posture convey a great deal. By being mindful of our non-verbal cues, we amplify our commitment to communion. For instance, reaching out to lightly touch someone's hand in a moment of vulnerability can signify deep empathy and solidarity.

Moreover, we can incorporate journaling as a tool to enhance our listening skills and promote communal understanding. After a conversation, reflecting on both our thoughts and the other person's message can reveal subconscious biases or assumptions we hold. Writing about our experiences allows us to process our emotions and analyse how we can engage more meaningfully in future dialogues.

Remember, listening to engage in communion fosters a culture of respect—and respect is a vital foundation for any relationship. When we enter conversations with the mindset of fostering understanding, we enhance our ability to connect genuinely. Recognising that everyone has a unique story enriches our awareness and deepens our relational capacity.

As we delve deeper into mastering communion through active listening, it is crucial to address the barriers that may impede our ability to listen effectively. Preconceptions, biases, and habitual patterns of dialogue can hinder our capacity to engage fully. Self-awareness is key in this process; acknowledging our emotional triggers, judgments, and distractions empowers us to step aside and focus on what truly matters—connecting with the other person.

A profound aspect of communion is the recognition that listening is a skill that can be honed through practice. Just like any other skill, improvement comes with deliberate effort and reflection. Engaging regularly in active listening exercises can enhance our ability to listen effectively. For example, dedicating time each week to engage in conversations where our sole focus is listening can reinforce this practice. We may consider attending workshops or seminars focused on communication skills, as these venues provide opportunities to learn from experts and practice with peers.

Engaging in communion fosters gratitude for the insights gained through the act of listening. We may often find that through our conversations, we receive answers and perspectives we did not know we were seeking. This humility to learn from others fosters a spirit of collaboration and communal growth.

In closing, engaging in communion through the practice of active listening is an essential skill that enriches our relationships and deepens our connections. The journey toward mastering this art involves patience, empathy, vulnerability, and a commitment to being present. By creating a safe space for dialogue, embracing our shared humanity, and valuing the act of listening, we can foster a culture of understanding—one conversation at a time.

Furthermore, it is vital to remember that the foundation of meaningful interactions lies in our intentions. As we approach each conversation, we must ground ourselves in the desire to connect and to grow together. When we listen not just with our ears but with our hearts, we amplify the power of our words and illuminate the shared narratives of our lives.

Let us continue to engage in communion, recognising that every conversation is an opportunity to bridge the gap between our souls. In this journey of listening, we become more than mere speakers; we become nurturers of connection and ambassadors of love, embodying the essence of faith through our words and actions.

Beyond Sound: Truly Living the Power of Words

Integrating Insights into Daily Life

As we reach the final stretch of our journey together, it becomes increasingly crucial to distil the insights we have gathered throughout this exploration of the power of words. The profound revelations about our communication—whether they serve to uplift, heal, or hinder—demand our thoughtful reflection and active application. It's one thing to understand the theoretical implications of mindful speech and heartfelt dialogue; it is another to weave these lessons into the very fabric of our daily interactions.

In this final subchapter, we will explore actionable strategies that enable you to integrate the wisdom imparted in this book into your everyday life. You'll find practical steps to transform your speech into a vessel of encouragement, connection, and love. The journey ahead calls for intentionality; therefore, let us embark on this exploration of integrating insights into daily life, recognising that the art of communication can profoundly shape not only our relationships but who we are as individuals.

Reflect and Review

Before applying these strategies, take a moment to review the foundational concepts we have discussed. What themes resonated with you the most? Were there any particular anecdotes or biblical principles that struck a chord in your heart? By engaging in this reflective practice, you will gain a deeper understanding of how your current communication style aligns with your values and the divine intentions you aspire to embody.

A reflective practice can be as simple as journaling or meditating on critical lessons learned. Consider setting aside a few minutes each day or week to ponder the following questions:

- How do my words reflect my identity in Christ?
- In what situations do I find it challenging to communicate positively?
- How can I frame my speech in a manner that aligns with my faith and serves those around me?

Mapping out your thoughts not only clarifies your understanding but also prepares you for the transformation that lies ahead.

Mindful Engagement

One paramount strategy for integrating insights into daily life is the practice of mindful engagement. This involves fully focusing on the present moment, genuinely listening to others, and considering the impact of your words before speaking. Mindful engagement encourages you to pause and reflect on your speech, ensuring it aligns with the principles of love, respect, and unity you have learned.

Begin each conversation to uplift. Take a deep breath before speaking, assessing your emotional state and the context of the exchange. Are you encountering tension? Is there an underlying need for empathy? By cultivating a habit of mindfulness, you transition from a reactionary communication style into a deliberative one that fosters understanding.

Practising active listening is also a vital component of mindful engagement. As you listen, maintain eye contact, nod in acknowledgement, and refrain from planning your response while the other person speaks. This shows that you value their words and perspective, creating an atmosphere of trust and openness.

Harness the Power of Affirmation

Throughout this book, we have emphasised the significance of affirmation—how the words we choose can encourage not just others but also ourselves. An effective way to integrate this into daily life is by consciously weaving affirmations into your conversations.

Start small by selecting specific affirmations that resonate with you. Think of biblical verses or positive declarations that uphold the virtues of faith, love, and kindness. For instance, phrases like 'I believe in your strength' or 'Your efforts matter' can go a long way in reinforcing the value of those around you.

Make it a habit to infuse conversations, both significant and mundane, with affirmations. Whether you are encouraging a friend going through a tough time or celebrating a colleague's success, your words can be agents of hope and positivity. To help you cultivate this skill, consider keeping a journal of affirmations or creating a list to draw from as needed. This serves as both a reminder and a guide in moments when genuine encouragement is necessary.

Create a Culture of Openness

Another essential strategy for integrating insights into daily life is fostering a culture of openness within your relationships. Establish an environment where honesty and vulnerability are not only welcomed but celebrated. By doing so, you foster a landscape in which your insights can flourish, and your conversations carry the weight of empathy and compassion.

To nurture such an environment, lead by example. Share your experiences, vulnerabilities, and lessons learned, allowing others to feel safe in expressing themselves without fear of judgment. Open-ended questions, such as 'What are you feeling about this situation?'

or 'How can I support you better?' can encourage deeper dialogue and connection.

Additionally, cultivate a practice of gratitude in your daily interactions. Express appreciation regularly, highlighting specific actions or traits you value in others. Cultivating a culture of gratitude not only strengthens relationships but also reinforces the emotional bond nurtured through honest communication.

Engage in Regular Check-Ins

To maintain the transformative practices you learn, consider setting up regular check-ins with yourself and the people in your life. This could be a weekly meeting with a friend or family member, or even a personal reflection at the end of the day. The purpose is to assess how well you are embodying the insights discussed and to adapt as necessary.

During these check-ins, evaluate how your communication aligns with your intentions. Are there moments when you fell short? Celebrate the successes and acknowledge the areas for growth. Genuine interest in the well-being of others, coupled with self-awareness, enhances both relational depth and clarity in speech. Remember, progress is a journey, not perfection—a gentle reminder that growth takes time and requires patience and understanding.

Embrace Opportunities for Vulnerability

Vulnerability has been a recurring theme in our exploration of encouragement and communication. Embracing opportunities to be vulnerable allows you to build deeper connections and fosters an atmosphere of authenticity.

Make it a goal to share your thoughts and feelings honestly, especially in situations where this openness may not come naturally. It's essential to acknowledge that vulnerability is not a weakness; rather, it is a sign of strength. When you speak from your heart, you permit others to do the same, creating a ripple effect of genuine connection.

For example, if you're feeling apprehensive about a significant life decision, discuss your emotions related to it with a trusted friend. Your choice to share your fears or uncertainties can reinforce that you value their perspective, encouraging them to open up in similar ways.

Align Your Words with Your Actions

In all interpersonal engagements, it is critical to remember that our words must align with our actions. The authenticity of our speech becomes credible only when it is reflected in how we live our daily lives. Therefore, integrate the values of kindness, compassion, and encouragement into your actions, ensuring they align with your spoken words.

For instance, if you commit to being more supportive, actively seek ways to demonstrate that support through your actions. Offer assistance, lend an ear, or simply be present. Let your words embody your intentions, deepening your credibility and nourishing trust in your relationships.

Cultivate Group Conversations

Transforming individual practices into collective actions amplifies their impact. Organise group conversations or gatherings focused on communication and encouragement. Share the insights gathered from this book and invite others to do the same.

Such gatherings serve as safe spaces for individuals to share their experiences, challenges, and victories in navigating the complexities of communication. Encourage participants to explore the themes of vulnerability, affirmation, and empathy in depth with one another. This collective dynamic fosters accountability and strengthens your shared commitment to mindful communication through the power of words.

Utilise Social Media with Intention

In a world increasingly dominated by digital communication, the role of social media cannot be overlooked. Be intentional about how you use social media platforms as a means of expression. Consider this space an extension of your voice and your values.

Use your platforms to share uplifting messages, scriptural insights, and positive affirmations. Engage with your audience by asking thought-provoking questions and encouraging them to share their experiences and stories. In doing so, you create a digital community centred on affirmation and connection rather than negativity and divisiveness.

Moreover, be mindful of the type of content you consume. Avoid inflammatory or discouraging narratives that could detract from the positive outlook you are striving to embody. Instead, follow accounts that inspire you, bring joy, and encourage growth.

Commit to Lifelong Learning

Finally, one of the most significant commitments you can make as you integrate the power of words into your life is to embrace lifelong learning. Cultivate a heart open to continued growth and exploration, recognising that the journey of understanding communication is ongoing.

Join workshops or classes that focus on developing communication skills. Read books or engage with podcasts that delve into themes of effective dialogue, emotional intelligence, and the power of words. Attend church seminars or discussion groups that explore biblical principles related to speech and relationships.

By committing to lifelong learning, you equip yourself with new tools and insights that can deepen your practice of meaningful communication and positively impact your relationships.

A Call to Action

As we conclude this book, I invite you to embrace the transformative journey that lies ahead. Recognise that the insights gathered are not merely theoretical notions but practical wisdom meant to be woven into the fabric of your life. Each conversation you engage in holds the potential to foster deeper relationships, reflect God's love, and inspire those around you.

Let us remember that the words we choose, the intention behind our communication, and the relationships we build are all part of a divine tapestry woven together to bring light and love into our world. As you step forward, carry the intention to speak life—fostering hope, joy, and encouragement wherever you go.

Ultimately, may your journey with words illuminate not only your life but also the lives of others, leading to a legacy of love and understanding that echoes through generations to come. Your words possess power—use them wisely, embody them authentically, and may they be a reflection of the beauty found in divine communication.

As you step out into the world, remember the indelible mark you can leave with every word spoken and every heart touched. Speak life, and let your voice be a beacon of encouragement, reflecting the essence of God's love in all that you do.

Embodying Transformative Practices

As we stand at the intersection of our beliefs and our words, it becomes clear that the communication we engage in shapes not only our relationships but also our very selves. In this transformative journey of embracing the power of words, we are called to create a personal action plan—a blueprint that outlines practical steps for integrating the principles of mindful speaking and intentional interactions into our lives.

To begin this journey, let us reflect on the core values that undergird our communication. These values serve as the foundation upon which our action plan will be built. As believers, we are called to communicate with love, grace, humility, and respect. It is through these values that our words can become a conduit for building connections that mirror our faith. The apostle Paul, in Colossians 4:6, exhorts us to let our speech be seasoned with grace, indicating that our words should not only convey meaning but also reflect the heart of God.

Therefore, an action plan will not merely consist of techniques and tips; it must also be deeply rooted in self-awareness and an understanding of our motivations and desires. With that in mind, let us embark on the journey of creating a personal action plan for embodying transformative practices in our communication.

1. Self-Reflection and Assessment

The first step requires a deliberate pause for self-reflection. Consider your recent conversations, both in personal and professional settings. Ask yourself:

- How do my words reflect my values and beliefs?
- Are there patterns in my communication that need to be addressed?
- Do I often speak words of encouragement or criticism?
- How do my words impact my relationships?

Keeping a journal can be beneficial during this phase. Write down specific interactions that stood out to you over the past week. Identify moments where your words fostered connection and instances where they may have created distance. Reflect upon your intentions in those moments—were they aligned with your desire to communicate effectively and compassionately?

2. Set Intentional Goals

Once you have undertaken self-reflection, the next step is to set intentional and achievable communication goals. Think of these goals as guiding stars; they will help steer you in the right direction as you navigate your interactions.

Goals can be categorised into short-term and long-term objectives:

- Short-term goals could include specifics such as:
- Practising active listening in conversations for the next week to foster deeper connections.
- Making a conscious effort to share one uplifting message daily, whether through spoken word or text.
- Replacing at least one negative statement in a conversation each day with an affirmation or a positive observation.
- Long-term goals might encompass broader aspirations such as:
- Cultivating a reputation for being a source of encouragement in both your personal and professional networks over the next six months.
- Committing to a year-long journey of studying various biblical principles regarding communication and applying them in your everyday life.

Setting goals not only provides direction but also gives you measurable checkpoints to assess your progress.

3. Developing Communication Techniques

With clear goals in place, the next step is to equip yourself with specific communication techniques to help you realise these objectives. Here are several techniques designed to promote mindful communication:

- Active Listening: This technique involves giving full attention to the speaker, resisting the urge to formulate a response while they're still talking. Instead, focus on understanding their message. You could ask clarifying questions or summarise their points to confirm your understanding.

- Mindful Pausing: Before responding in a conversation, take a moment to breathe deeply. This brief yet impactful pause enables you to gather your thoughts and respond more deliberately, rather than react impulsively.
- Positive Affirmation: Make it a habit to affirm others during conversations. For instance, when a colleague shares an idea, acknowledge their effort before offering constructive feedback.
- Empathy Statements: Incorporate phrases that convey understanding and empathy into your conversations. Phrases such as 'I can see how that would be difficult' or

'It sounds like you're feeling overwhelmed' can help create a supportive environment.

- Nonverbal Communication Awareness: Pay attention to body language and nonverbal cues. Ensure that your actions align with your words, as this consistency builds trust and authenticity.

Practising these techniques intentionally will gradually transform your communication habits over time.

4. Engaging in accountability

The journey of embodying transformative practices is most successful when supported by accountability and follow-through. Finding an accountability partner or group can significantly enhance your commitment to achieving your goals. Consider the following options:

- Partnership with a Friend: Share your communication goals with a trusted friend or family member. Regularly check in with one another to discuss progress, challenges, and moments of success.
- Joining a Support Group: Participate in a group focused on personal growth and effective communication. Here, individuals share insights, provide feedback, and encourage one another to stay on course.

- Professional Guidance: If appropriate, seek out a coach, mentor, or counsellor specialising in communication. They can provide personalised strategies, insights, and tools based on their expertise.

Accountability encourages perseverance; it is through shared encouragement that we become empowered to grow and develop.

5. Regular Review and Reflection

Transformative practices flourish with consistent review and reflection. Schedule weekly or monthly check-ins with yourself to assess your progress. During these sessions, revisit your goals and evaluate whether you've been able to implement the techniques you set out to practice. Ask yourself:

- What successes have I experienced in my communication this past week or month?
- Have I faced any challenges, and how did I respond to them?
- What new insights have I gained about my communication habits?

This reflective practice serves as a powerful tool for reinforcing positive changes and recognising areas for ongoing improvement.

6. Embracing Continuous Learning

As we develop our communication skills, the journey is ongoing. Embrace the principle of continuous learning as a means to deepen your understanding of effective communication. Consider:

- Engaging with Books and Resources: Explore literature, podcasts, and workshops that centre around mindful communication. Many renowned authors offer valuable insights that can broaden your understanding of the world.
- Practising Different Perspectives: In conversations, strive to view situations from multiple angles. This practice fosters empathy and enables more nuanced conversations.
- Learning from Mistakes: Understand that miscommunication will happen. Rather than avoiding it, embrace mistakes as opportunities for growth. Reflect on the experience and consider what adjustments can enhance your future interactions.

7. Cultivating a Heart of Gratitude

Finally, we must not underestimate the power of gratitude in our communication. Cultivating a heart of gratitude aligns our actions with a mindset of appreciation, thereby enhancing our interactions with others. Consider integrating these practices:

- Gratitude Journaling: Maintain a journal where you note specific people or interactions you are grateful for each day. Reflecting on these positive experiences can remind you of the importance of your words and the value of communication.
- Sharing Gratitude: Regularly express gratitude to others in your life. A simple thank you, a compliment, or an acknowledgement of their impact can uplift their spirit while reinforcing your commitment to positive communication.

Conclusion

The journey of embodying transformative practices in our communication is not a sprint, but a marathon—a continuous process that invites us to grow, learn, and engage authentically with one another. By following the steps outlined in this action plan, we can cultivate a vibrant communication style deeply rooted in our values and faith.

Through intentional speaking and mindful interactions, we have the power to illuminate the hearts of those around us, fostering relationships that reflect the love of the Creator. As we move forward, let us remember that our words hold weight—they can either build or tear down. May we choose wisely, embodying transformative practices that resonate with the truth of our faith and the depth of our commitment to speak life into every situation.

Let us commit to embracing this journey, being empowered by the knowledge that our words can change the world—for ourselves, our families, our communities, and ultimately, our relationship with God.

A Call to Action

As we stand at the crossroads of our journey through the transformative power of words, it is essential to recognise the magnitude of what we have explored together. Our words are not mere strings of letters or sounds; they are vessels of emotions, reflections of our spirits, and conduits of connection. Throughout this book, we have endeavoured to unravel the intricate relationship between communication, faith, and our interactions with one another. Now, as we come to a close, it is time to take the insights learned and transform them into action.

This is a call to action—an invitation to step boldly into the world with a renewed understanding of the weight our words carry and the impact they can make. It is about embracing the transformative journey that lies ahead of us. Each of us has the potential to be a beacon of hope, a source of encouragement, and an agent of change through the words we speak.

The Power of Words

To embark on this journey meaningfully, we must first understand that our words can either uplift or tear down. Every time we engage in conversation, we have the power to ignite passion and purpose or to sow seeds of doubt and frustration. The choice is ours, and with that choice comes a profound responsibility. From the smallest interactions to the more significant dialogues, we are called to be mindful of the effects our words have on those around us.

In our quest to speak life, we must commit to intentionality in our communication. This means choosing our words carefully, aligning them with our values, and ensuring that they reflect the love we wish to convey. Let's consider how we can begin this transformation journey today.

One of the first steps we can take is to cultivate a habit of positivity in our speech. This might mean starting your day with affirmations, reminding yourself of the truth of your identity and purpose. Consider incorporating Scripture into your daily affirmations, allowing the truth of God's Word to shape your perspective and, subsequently, your words. When we ground ourselves in the truth of who we are in God's eyes, we are more equipped to share that truth with those around us, fostering a culture of encouragement and love.

Next, we should focus on creating a dialogue that is rich in authenticity. Authenticity allows us to engage deeply and meaningfully with others. It is about being truthful in our expression, not simply conforming to societal expectations. When we speak from our true selves, we invite others to do the same. This shared vulnerability can open doors to genuine connection and profound relationship-building.

Consider the impact of intentional clarity in your conversations. Miscommunication can lead to misunderstandings and resentment. Therefore, take the time to express your thoughts clearly and ensure that your audience understands your intent. This clarity will facilitate healthier dialogues and foster a sense of trust and security. Encourage others to ask questions and seek clarification when necessary, creating an atmosphere where everyone feels free to express themselves without fear of judgment.

Moreover, let us not forget the importance of active listening in our conversations. Engaging fully with what others are saying not only honours their voice but also enriches your understanding. Listening allows for a deeper connection and demonstrates that we value the perspectives and feelings of others. Through active listening, we can respond more thoughtfully and meaningfully, ensuring that our words resonate well with those we interact with.

As we prepare to step into the world, let us also commit to embracing empathy in our conversations. Empathy serves as a bridge, connecting us with people from diverse backgrounds. When we empathise with others, we acknowledge their experiences and emotions, allowing our words to reflect understanding, compassion, and grace. This alignment of our speech with the experiences of others creates an atmosphere where healing and reconciliation can occur.

In practical terms, remember to be patient with yourself and others as you navigate this journey of mindful speech. Change takes time, and old habits are hard to break. When temptations to revert to negative speech arise, pause and reflect on what you want to communicate. Ask yourself how your words can align with love, faith, and encouragement. The effort to implement these practices will ultimately yield a harvest of deeper and more meaningful relationships.

But this journey transcends personal transformation; it extends to our communities. Begin by adopting small, measurable changes in your environment—whether it's your home, workplace, or social circles. Encourage your family members to speak to one another positively, fostering a culture where words are chosen carefully and with love. Utilise expressions of gratitude and appreciation as daily practices, reinforcing the notion that words hold incredible power.

In a work environment, rally your colleagues around the concept of constructive feedback. Develop a system where everyone feels comfortable sharing ideas, suggestions, and observations without fear of negative repercussions. This commitment to positivity and support will foster an environment that is ripe for collaboration and innovation, all rooted in open and mindful communication.

Additionally, engage with your community through your words. Participate in outreach programs that focus on uplifting those in need. Whether volunteering at a local food bank or supporting a community centre, use your words to encourage hope and inspire resilience. By speaking life into those who may feel marginalised or hopeless, you can make a profound difference in the lives of others and ignite change in your community.

As we reflect on what it means to live out the power of our words, we commit to being ambassadors of grace and hope. Speak life into every opportunity, whether through a smile, a kind word, or a listening ear. Understand the privilege it is to communicate with others—that each interaction presents a sacred opportunity to reflect God's love and truth.

Remember, we can create atmospheres of trust, understanding, and healing through our speech. By fostering relationships built on intentional, loving communication, we will not only see our lives transformed, but also those of those around us. The impact of our words can create cascading effects, rippling out into our families, communities, and the broader world.

The Power of Words

Let this be a commitment, a promise to ourselves and those we interact with: to speak with intention, purpose, and love. As we come together around this common goal, we can transform the very landscape of our interactions and create a world where encouragement, authenticity, and compassion reign supreme.

In closing, take a moment to reflect on the journey that lies ahead of you. Picture the conversations you will have, the connections you will foster, and the lives you will touch through the power of your words. Embrace this chance to become more than just a speaker; dare to become a voice of hope, a champion of love, and a catalyst for change.

Now, step forth into the world—armed with your newly honed abilities and a heart aligned with truth and love. Engage mindfully and inspire meaningfully. Together, we can wield the incredible power of our words, transforming them into instruments of light and life in all our relationships.

The Power of Words

Thank you, fabulous readers!

Wow! You made it to the end! Seriously, that's no small feat, and I'm genuinely thrilled to have had you along for this wild ride. Thank you for sharing your time with me as we explored the labyrinth of life through these pages! Each story told and idea discussed is a piece of a larger puzzle that reflects the complexity and beauty of our shared humanity. As you close this book, I hope you feel a little spark of excitement ignited within you. Go ahead and carry that feeling into your life, embracing the world with open arms and an open mind. Remember that what we discovered here can't be confined to these pages—it's meant to spill over into our everyday lives and inspire us to take action! I encourage you to share the revelations, insights, and laughter you found here. Talk about it with your friends, family, or that random person you encounter at the coffee shop. Let's make this more than just a book—it's a movement, a celebration of ideas that are waiting to burst forth into reality! Life is too short for silence, and your voice is powerful. And while this chapter ends, know that it's just the beginning of many more adventures, stories, and explorations waiting for us

The Power of Words

in the vast expanse of existence. Keep questioning, keep dreaming, and keep seizing each moment with the same intensity that fuelled the creation of this book. I can't express enough just how grateful I am for each of you who dared to dive into this journey with me. Until we meet again in the next adventure, may your days be filled with joy, curiosity, and endless possibilities.

Keep shining bright!

Daniel Meguille

www.ingramcontent.com/pod-product-compliance
Lightning Source LLC
Chambersburg PA
CBHW052018070526
44584CB00016B/1809